More Prais[e for] Ipswich On My Mind

"In Canada Bob is known as a great mentor to C-Suite executives. But as this collection demonstrates, his greatest strength is as a storyteller, in the mold of Canada's Stephen Leacock or America's Mark Twain. His writing is a delight."

—Jay Rosenzweig, CEO, Rosenzweig & Co., Toronto

"Every time I dip into one his columns, I am transported to a sunny porch in Ipswich on a Saturday morning, enjoying a cup of coffee and a chat with my friend Bob. It's quite magical."

—David Agnew, President, Seneca Polytechnic, Toronto

"Bob writes with humor, and a wry fondness for his hometown of Ipswich, all the more impressive as he does so from a considerable distance. On his regular return visits, he observes, reports, and remembers what it was like growing up here, sharing his thoughts and feelings in these excellent columns."

—David Updike, Teacher and Writer

"Bob evokes powerful memories while calling on us to fully appreciate all that surrounds us and enriches our lives right now. And how wonderful when it is accomplished with such gentle humor and grace."

—Steven Poskanzer, President Emeritus, Carleton College

"In an era of over-stuffed in-boxes, I somehow always find time to read Bob Waite's columns. Drawing on his personal experiences - from cub reporter to the pinnacles of politics and the business world - he shares personal stories of yesteryear that often provoke unexpected observations about current issues. And there are always laughs - lots of them!"

—Mike Petersen, Board Chair, BDC;
former Group Head, U.S. Banking, TD

"Having grown up in Ipswich with Bobby, we share a wonderful history in this town. His essays enlighten, educate, and amuse, offering a bit of levity in these trying times. It is also the only time I can read about politics without grinding my teeth!"

—Ann Herrick Causey, Lifetime Friend

"Though I have never lived in Ipswich, Bob's columns make me wish I had. Some resonate personally — I was Bob's editor at Pacific News Service, which he mentions — but mostly I relish his dry wit, trenchant observations, and, of course, his fervid devotion to fried clams."

—Clark Norton, Expert in Baby-Boomer Travel

"Begin this irresistible, anecdotal book of joy, humor and heart and be drawn instantly into the past and present of Ipswich life and lives. The perfect book for those who love a good story and those who might otherwise never pick up a book."

—Mike McGrath, Zenobia Emporium

"If Ipswich is on your mind, you will surely enjoy this book. Bob Waite is a wonderful writer, an insightful memoirist, and a very funny man. Buy his book and I can assure you of many chuckles—even if Ipswich is far from your mind."

***—David Osborne, Author of* Reinventing Government**
The Coming, *and other book*

"Bob Waite grabs current events and intertwines them with life here in Ipswich. We always learn something new about ourselves, about our town, all through the lens of Bob's unique sense of humor. You will love this, his second book of fabulously entertaining essays."

—Frederic and Susan Winthrop, Conservationists

"Bob has the keen ability to portray Ipswich in a way that lures the outsider in yet keeps his "regulars" (i.e. townie friends) laughing their socks off. I have had the joy of watching Bob's fan club wait in line to have him sign their books. Ipswich loves him!"

—Betsy Frost, owner of the shop where Bob's book is the #1 Bestseller

"For my entire life, I've listened to my brother Bob weave the most fantastical stories around the life he's lived and the places he's been. However, in the case of *Ipswich Out of My Mind*, I can assure you they are mostly true!"

—Tom Waite, bestselling author of thrillers

"Bob Waite's story-telling is magical. Whimsy, deft descriptions, and wry wit define each page. You will love this book!"

—Sue Bright, who brought Bob to IBM Canada as chief speechwriter

"I have read all of Bob's columns and enjoy every one of them. You'll particularly love his self-deprecating sense of humour. But I still find myself checking his columns for typos or left out prepositions!"

—Pat Reilly, Bob's Executive Assistant at CIBC

"Anything that keeps Bob busy and out of trouble is a good thing."

—Karen Shigeishi-Waite, President, Waite + Co.

Ipswich Out Of My Mind

Also by Bob Waite

Green Bananas: Financial Fitness For Life (with Jeff Wachman)

Achieving Financial Fitness (with Jeff Wachman)

Conversations With John Updike (Chapter)

Ipswich On My Mind

Ipswich Out Of My Mind

More Amusing Musings About Life's Joys and Absurdities

Bob Waite

Marlborough Press

Boston

First Edition: September 2023

Cover: "Ipswich Shanties" Arthur Wesley Dow (courtesy of the Ipswich Museum; high resolution image by Stoney Stone)

Cover Design: Asha Hossain

Electronic and Print Formatting: Dallas Hodge

Font: *Glacial Indifference* – a sans serif typeface with inspirations from Bauhaus geometric fonts

Bob Waite Caricature: Ed Colley

ISBN: 978-0-9850258-4-7

Printed in the United States of America

For Karen, Joseph, and Emily

Table of Contents

Author's Note

It has been 55 years since Phillip K. Dick published "Do Androids Dream of Electric Sheep?" (and 41 years since director Ridley Scott translated that groundbreaking science fiction novel to the big screen as "Blade Runner").

It has been just one year since I published "Ipswich On My Mind".

In that short period Dick's vision of an age of thinking machines capable of feelings, memories and, yes, inklings of their own mortality, has drawn uncomfortably near. Artificial intelligence -AI - has become a buzzword that not only drives conversations, but stock valuations.

Its literary offspring, ChatGPT, has sent shockwaves through academia, from haughty Harvard to humble North Shore Community College. At the school where I teach, Seneca Polytechnic, the topic has stirred the greatest degree of faculty discomfort since the introduction of co-ed washrooms.

The good news is that Seneca survived co-ed washrooms, adapting so quickly that no one recalls what all the fuss was about. Perhaps that will be the same with ChatGPT and AI in general.

It is perhaps fitting that as I pen this Author's Note I am in Toronto, attending the Toronto International Film Festival, as I have done almost every year since the 1990's. What is different this time around is that much of the glitz and glitter are absent, due to a strike by screen writers and actors. The central issue between the creative community and the industry's producers and studios is – you guessed it – AI.

This book, save for a sonnet written in the manner of Shakespeare extolling the virtues of Ipswich's championship high school girl's varsity volleyball team, is completely ChatGPT-free. Further, I can attest that no androids of any kind were harmed in its compilation.

Its title – "Ipswich Out Of My Mind" – suggests the book as companion to "Ipswich On My Mind", which of course it is. And while my first book's title consciously drew on Willie Nelson's sense of longing and memory (tinged with regret), the second might conceivably be linked by some to the Rolling Stones album "Out of Our Heads".

Like the first, this book is a product of memory, rooted in a place, Ipswich. But its intent is to range far and wide in terms of topic and to deal with contemporary issues as well as those rooted in the past. The cover of both books claims to contain "amusing musings". Whether or not they achieve that is best left to the individual reader to decide. But I do hope some find the writing thought-provoking, and if an occasional chuckle escapes, so much the better.

I returned to column writing after a 40-year hiatus at the behest of the late Bill Wasserman, my first publisher. At the age of 92, he and John Muldoon had, against all logic, launched a newspaper, *Ipswich Local News.* Soon afterwards Bill, in an email, wondered if I could still string sentences together sensibly "remembering the humor you were once known for."

Bill never failed to know which button to push. I of course took up the challenge, as he knew I would.

As with the first book, the proceeds of "Ipswich Out Of My Mind" will go to benefit reader-supported, community-driven journalism in the form of *Ipswich Local News.* It is the least I can do for the community I love and the profession I never really left.

— Bob Waite, Toronto, September 8, 2023

Foreword

When Bob asked me to write an introduction to his second book, my first reaction was to procrastinate. When he emailed a gentle reminder, my follow-up reaction was to promise a delivery date ... then procrastinate some more.

All of which is the exact opposite to Bob's work schedule. He gets his work in weeks in advance and leaves me sitting on a small cache of future columns.

But what I really like is reading them. Seeing a new Bob Waite column drop into my mailbox is one of the high points of my week.

As a relative newcomer to town, I particularly enjoy his humorous recollections of times gone by. When he's recalling a hideous high school woodworking project thrown over the County Street Bridge or a young boy telling very tall tales at the Whipple House, Bob connects us with the past. Doing it in the pages of the *Ipswich Local News*, he makes it a shared experience.

Bob tackles many other topics, of course. As a former press secretary for Senators Ed Brooke of Massachusetts and Bob Dole of Kansas, our Bob has a lifetime of political experience to draw upon.

Whether he's exploring the quirks of small-town life, pondering the mysteries of what happened to normal politics, or reflecting on the challenges of human relationships, Bob's columns offer a unique perspective on the world we inhabit.

In an era when the news cycle moves at a breakneck pace and national headlines often focus on the sensational and the divisive, Bob Waite's columns provide a welcome respite — a chance to slow down, to savor the written word, and to rediscover the joy of storytelling.

Bob's columns are a testament to the enduring power of storytelling and a reminder that, in the hands of a skilled wordsmith, the written word has the ability to inspire, to uplift, and to connect us all.

As you embark through Bob's book, please bear in mind that proceeds go to support the non-profit *Ipswich Local News*, a project Bob has supported wholeheartedly since it was first founded in 2019.

John P. Muldoon

Editor and Publisher

Ipswich Local News

Get your thrills from the sea on Route 133

While many Americans back in the day were getting their kicks on Route 66, I was getting my thrills from the sea on Route 133. That's Massachusetts Route 133 — specifically the section running from Ipswich to Essex, Massachusetts, known as the "Clam Highway."

This nine-mile stretch of road links two historic colonial towns with a shared passion for harvesting and serving up seafood, in particular the fried clam.

My connection with this highway runs long and deep.

When I was growing up in Ipswich it ran directly past my home. For one brief period as a kid, I used to make terrifying 6 a.m. runs along the twisting roadway from Ipswich to Gloucester to retrieve huge blocks of ice for Grant's Seafood, one of the town's many seafood restaurants.

I was about 14. Mr. Grant was about 55 – and he drove his overloaded truck at about 80 mph. At 6 a.m., he explained, the Essex police would be eating donuts at the Village restaurant, so no need to worry.

Later I was the food critic for six area newspapers. Writing under the pseudonym Colleen Smacznego (Smacznego means "enjoy your meal" in Polish), I visited and reviewed restaurants from the Clam Box in Ipswich to J.T. Farnham's in Essex – and all those in between.

You can't miss the Clam Box restaurant in Ipswich, built to resemble the real thing

Ipswich and Essex, located on the "shoulder" of Cape Ann, north of Boston, was once one town. Essex broke off from Ipswich in 1819. But topographically, both remain linked by extensive salt marshes and access to the all-important clam flats – and, of course, Route 133.

The clam in question is soft-shelled and is most often eaten either steamed ("steamers") or fried with its "whole-belly" intact. While called "Ipswich" clams, similar bi-valve molluscs are also sourced from Maine and Maryland. The largest distributor is Ipswich Shellfish, whose yellow-and-blue trucks can be seen all along the East Coast.

A local rival company, Soffron Brothers, specialized in "clam strips" – created by harvesting a "belly-less" section from the far larger, hard-shelled sea clam. For more than 30 years, Soffron had an exclusive contract to supply scores of Howard Johnson restaurants with clam strips.

The origin of the fried clam is a matter of dispute. According to Essex folks, it was concocted by Lawrence "Chubby" Woodman, who, on July 3, 1916, dredged some whole-bellied clams in corn meal, fried them up in lard and created a culinary item that no less an authority than Howard Johnson would later proclaim to be "sweet as a nut."

Woodman's claims this is the origin story of the "New England Fried Clam."

Woodman's lays claim to have invented the fried clam, but there are dissenters in Ipswich

Not unexpectedly, Ipswich people take exception.

According to "Stories from the River's Mouth" by Sam Sherman, "True Ipswich clams were fried by Honey Russell and served at Russell's Lunch." While Sherman cites no exact date, the implication is that this, too, happened in 1916 — and that by using "corn flour, not corn meal," Russell had invented the "true Ipswich clam."

As an Ipswich native, I suppose I should care about this, but to me it's just a tempest in a deep fryer.

One of my favorite places to get fried clams is in Ipswich – the Clam Box. It is north of the town center and can't be missed, as it looks exactly like the boxes take-out clams have traditionally been served in.

Founded in 1935, the current structure was erected in 1938 and has become a regional landmark. Their mantra is "We don't claim to have invented the fried clam, but we perfected it."

Established by one of the many Greek-American families involved in the local seafood industry, they've done a pretty good job of fulfilling that promise. My preference is to order a full plate with a side dish of coleslaw and some onion rings; but a clam roll is an excellent option for those looking for a bit less.

Another good place for fried clams in Ipswich is the Choate Bridge Pub, located near America's oldest stone arch bridge, which spans the Ipswich River.

Here you are more likely to be among locals – and have access to local and national brews. And the Ipswich Clambake Company on High Street gets good reviews.

Views of the marshlands from Farnham's

In Essex, Woodman's is certainly a must – and it offers the kind of fun "in the rough" family dining experience that many associate with clam and lobster "shacks" of old.

However, if you are looking for something a bit more refined, the Village Restaurant up the street is a good choice – it is the place I take my three sisters when we want seafood.

But in reality, there are many good choices between the two towns. For example, Farnham's in Essex, while only open between March and December, offers one of the most spectacular marshland views you'll find anywhere on the East Coast.

Now I know what you might be thinking at this point – do I really want to go all that way just for a lunch or dinner?

My answer is that you might come for the clams – but you'll want to stay for the two towns' history, their scenic beauty, and Crane, one of the best white-sand beaches anywhere.

A clammer at low tide. Photo from Historic Ipswich.

If flying, Ipswich and Essex are most easily accessed from airports in Boston or Manchester, New Hampshire. While there is MBTA train service to Ipswich from Boston, your best bet is to rent a vehicle.

For accommodation, there are several good places. We enjoy Kaede Bed and Breakfast atop Town Hill in Ipswich. Located in a large 1845 Federalist-period structure, the hosts offer New England hospitality with a Japanese accent. I often stay at The Ipswich Inn Bed & Breakfast – famous for its friendly staff, excellent breakfasts, and tolerance for well-behaved dogs. The Inn at Castle Hill is pricier but puts you closer to the sea and beach.

If you decide to stay in Essex and would like a true colonial experience, the 1695 Cedar Hill Farm Bed and Breakfast might be just the ticket (don't worry – they have all the modern amenities).

But with any restaurant or inn, given the waxing and waning COVID-19 restrictions, it is best to check ahead. Tell them Colleen Smacznego sent you.

Have a Devil of a Time in Ipswich

According to legend, Ipswich's "Devil's Footprint" was formed when Satan leaped off a local church steeple. Photo from Historic Ipswich.

You can have a devil of a time in Ipswich, Massachusetts. Or at least the residents apparently did back in the 1740's.

According to local legend, a visit by a famous English fire-and-brimstone preacher, the Rev. George Whitfield, to the town's First Congregational Church, located atop Town Hill, attracted a huge crowd – and a curious Satan.

Whitfield, who had no sympathy for the devil, called Satan out. Their raucous confrontation ended with them at the top of the church's steeple, where Whitfield delivered a denunciation so powerful that it caused the devil to jump…and leave his footprint forever imprinted in the rock below.

Or so the story goes.

Another version of the devil – in the form of Jack Nicholson – visited the town for the making of "The Witches of Eastwick," the film adaptation of the John Updike novel. Updike, who spent his most productive years as an Ipswich resident, also penned "Couples," a thinly veiled parable of the joys and pitfalls of small-town infidelity. The book ends with a later incarnation of the First Church burning to the ground – as it actually did in 1965.

Fortunately, while there have been six First Church structures on Meetinghouse Green on Town Hill, most of the town's colonial heritage – and that of nearby Essex – has remained intact.

In contrast to nearby places like Salem and Newburyport, whose deeper harbors facilitated maritime trade (and fueled renewal), Ipswich's silted river mouth and sand bars left it something of a backwater.

Jack Nicholson as a hungry Devil in the film "Witches of Eastwick," shot in Ipswich. Warner Bros. photo

So where others replaced so-called First Period (pre-1725) structures, Ipswichites made do with an occasional fresh coat of paint or the odd addition. The result is that the town boasts more First Period houses than any other community in America.

While most of the houses can only be viewed from the outside, one — the John Whipple House (1677) — is open to the public and well worth a visit. Among other things, note the width of the floorboards, a testament to the old-growth forest encountered by the first settlers.

Led by John Winthrop, Jr., son of the colonial governor, about a dozen men arrived in 1633 and set about building crude dwellings near today's town wharf as well as a Puritan Meeting House on the same high hill where the sixth version stands today.

If colonial history is your thing, I would highly recommend walking tours offered by a local fellow named Gordon Harris. I took one with my family and was amazed by how much I didn't know about a place where I grew up and worked as a journalist. The tour is not overly strenuous, lasts a couple of hours and typically begins and ends at the Ipswich Public Library.

Another place worth a stop is the Essex Shipbuilding Museum. Essex produced more wooden fishing schooners than any other place between 1668 and the 20th century, and this museum, located in the historic A.D. Story shipyard, offers both exhibits and live demonstrations.

You may recognize Ipswich's Castle Hill-Great House complex as the location for various films: it also hosts a popular summer concert series. Trustees of Reservations photo.

If your tastes run more to recreation and outdoor activities, Ipswich and Essex offer ample opportunities in stunning settings.

In Ipswich, Crane Beach and its adjacent Castle Hill-Great House complex are the top attractions. The beach and mansion grounds were once owned by the Crane family of Chicago, who made their fortune by operating a foundry and manufacturing plumbing supplies, including sinks, toilets and the like. Today both are owned and managed by the non-profit Trustees of Reservations.

Crane beach features miles of white sand and dunes and, thanks to one of those sand bars, relatively calm swimming. Calm, but chilly – it typically takes until late August for the water temperature to approach 70.

Castle Hill and its Great House have formed the backdrop for several films – most notably the aforementioned "Witches of Eastwick" and Greta Gerwig's "Little Women" (2019) – while the beach was featured in "The Thomas Crown Affair" (1968) starring Steve McQueen and Faye Dunaway. Castle Hill also hosts a popular outdoor summer concert series, which dates back to the 1950's.

Although Ipswich today has a population of about 14,000 (and Essex about 3,750), both feel spacious as so much of the land is protected marshlands, beach reservation, or open fields.

Crane Beach is beautiful but watch out for high parking fees and seasonal greenhead flies. Trustees of Reservations photo.

One of the best ways to explore these open vistas is by kayak or canoe. The Ipswich River presents one opportunity – Foote Brothers have been renting canoes on the river for decades and a paddle upriver or down takes you into the tranquility of two state parks and a wildlife sanctuary.

If salt water is more your thing, you can rent a kayak from Crane Estate Kayak Adventures and paddle in the area behind Crane Beach. In either case, you will be rewarded with natural beauty (and, if you are a birder, a chance to knock a few more species off your life list).

Another way to enjoy the out-of-doors is to visit Appleton Farms. Established in 1638 and maintained by nine generations of the same family, it is one of the oldest continuously operating farms in North America.

The 1,000 acres are now managed by the Trustees of Reservations and offer access to walking trails as well as farm-fresh goods for sale in their store. The farm still operates in a traditional manner – so watch out for cow pies!

Whether your interests run to history, beach-going, kayaking — or clams — Ipswich and Essex have a lot to offer. But plan ahead – remember, the devil is in the details!

If You Go

If you are interested in a Gordon Harris historic walking tour, he can be contacted via the Historic Ipswich website. There is a modest charge.

Be aware that non-residents are assessed a parking fee of $45 per vehicle at Crane Beach. Also, for about three weeks during the summer (typically late July to early August) the beach and salt marshes are visited by the dreaded greenhead fly. There are no refunds at the beach, so check things out first.

If you are looking for cuisine (other than fried clams and other seafood), Riverview Pizza in Ipswich is a personal favorite – try the kielbasa pizza, which reflects the establishment's Polish heritage. For traditional New England fare, Ipswich's 1640 Hart House is an excellent choice – my family has gathered there for generations for special events and has yet to be disappointed.

When you live next to a cemetery, you never know who might come knocking at your door

The cast of MASH (CBS publicity photo)

When you live next to a cemetery, you never know who might knock at your door.

The cemetery in question is the Old South. Our house nestled up against it, and a portion of our land, lightly wooded, wrapped around the back of the old burial ground, eventually falling away towards the river.

This particular knock came in May of 1968. It was a somewhat agitated middle-aged woman, Marileeds Heard Chamberlain. She was very much to the point.

Her husband had just died in a terrible car accident. She wanted him buried in the Heard family plot but had learned that a portion of it — the very portion they wanted to use — was technically on our land. Would we cede it to her?

My dad, at first startled by the request, acquiesced.

And that is how Dr. John Maxwell Chamberlain got laid to rest on our land. Or what had been our land.

Growing up next door to the Old South, you became quite familiar with its residents — the Choates, Appletons, Kinsmans, Lakemans, and others who had family plots.

The cemetery at this point was "closed" — no room at the inn. Unless you were, like Dr. Chamberlain, grandfathered in.

Fast-forward exactly a decade. I am the newly-minted managing editor of *North Shore Sunday*, a weekend newspaper launched by our own Bill Wasserman and Canadian-American billionaire Mort Zuckerman.

One of my reporters, reassigned by Bill from his Danvers paper, is Brooke Chamberlain Pope.

She is a solid journalist, particularly adept at teasing out human-interest stories. But it was her own family story that I found fascinating.

It was her mother who had knocked at our door. It was her father, Dr. Chamberlain, who inhabited the newly-annexed stretch of ground a few steps from our house.

Over many weeks I gradually learned a great deal about Dr. Chamberlain. He went by the name "Max."

He practiced medicine (thoracic surgery) in Manhattan, commuting on weekends to the North Shore.

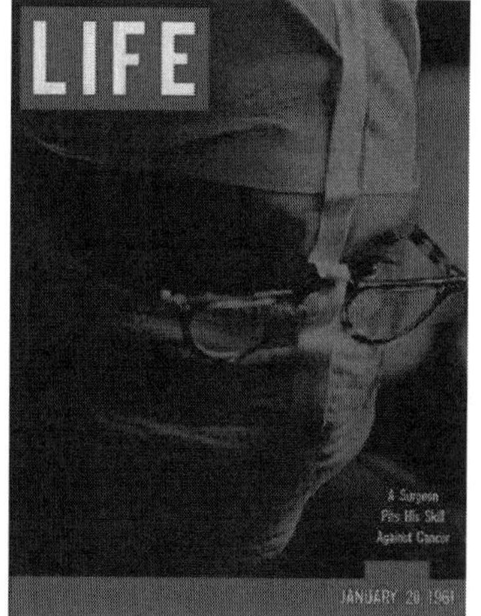

On January 20, 1961, he had been on the cover of *Life* magazine and profiled in an article, "A surgeon pits his skill against cancer," by W.C. Heinz.

Not that you would recognize him. In the cover photo, he is fully masked and wearing a surgical cap, his piercing eyes framed by horn-rimmed glasses.

Heinz later published a book, *The Surgeon*, which drew on his observations of Chamberlain.

It was that book that led to Chamberlain's most culturally consequential act, serving as a kind of midwife to the creation of *M*A*S*H*, the Robert Altman film that subsequently became one of the most successful TV series of all time.

In 1967, barely a year before his death, Chamberlain received a letter from a former student, Hiester Richard Hornberger, lamenting that he had been working for 11 years on a novel about his experiences as a Korean War M*A*S*H unit surgeon but had failed to find a publisher.

Hornberger did not hide his desperation: "That clown who wrote your book might be interested that I have a book I put together from my experiences in Korea."

Dr. Chamberlain passed the book along to the "clown" — Heinz — who agreed to become co-author and whipped the manuscript into publishable shape. They used a pseudonym, Richard Hooker. The rest is history.

The novel did well. The film version did better still. And the TV series ran for 11 seasons, was nominated for 109 Emmys (winning 14) and 22 Golden Globes (winning eight).

Its finale, airing on February 28, 1983, was the most viewed in broadcast history.

Dr. Chamberlain, of course, never lived to see any of this. In a poignant reminder of the frailty of life, the great cancer surgeon had himself been diagnosed with the dread disease, advanced to the point of inoperability.

Perhaps knowing all too well what lay ahead, there were no skid marks before his vehicle hit a parkway abutment that May day. He died, age 62.

But in the simple act of passing along a student's manuscript, he in some ways found immortality.

(Bob went on to live next to a cemetery in Toronto for 17 years.)

Trying to be funny in today's woke world is no laughing matter

Ricky Gervais (publicity photo)

In his own quiet way, my uncle Neil Bennett was a funny guy.

He was chair of the English Department at Vanderbilt University. Back in the 1970s, he asked me if I knew why discussions among academics were so acrimonious and vicious.

I said I did not.

"Because the stakes are so small," he deadpanned.

Uncle Neil received his doctorate from Yale and was considered the leading authority on American novelist William Dean Howells. I once asked him why he picked Howells.

He replied, "Someone had to."

When I was living in Nashville, a group of us, including Uncle Neil, went to see a new Mel Brooks film *Blazing Saddles.* He loved Mel Brooks. And he loved *Blazing Saddles.*

There comes a scene in the movie where the white railroad construction foreman admits he will hire anyone of any racial or ethnic background (using politically incorrect names for African Americans, Hispanics, Italians, and Jews), "… but **NOT** the Irish!"

Did I mention that Bennett is an Irish name?

As this line was delivered, I could see out of the corner of my eye my uncle, a man whom many took to be a paragon of academic propriety and rectitude, rolling around in the aisle, laughing hysterically.

Again, during the 70s, according to his son Shaun, Uncle Neil would impishly ask, "How many feminists does it take to change a light bulb?"

Keep in mind that at this point the women's movement had been fully launched. And that his wife, my Aunt JoAnn, was a fully liberated woman.

This was extremely dangerous turf.

But people took the bait. "How many?"

"One," my uncle would reply. "And it's **NOT** funny!"

Which, of course, was an unexpected punchline — and thus very funny indeed.

Figuring out what is funny and what is off limits nowadays is becoming increasingly difficult.

For example, more than a year ago I wrote a column poking fun at the "slow children" signs scattered around town. My spouse, God bless her, had noticed one close to my family's former home on Manning Street, as well as one near our later house on South Village Green.

She was not the first of my out-of-town friends to spy these signs (and to suggest they were posted to expose my intellectual shortcomings). This seemed useful fodder for some self-deprecatory humor, so I used it as the basis of a column.

The column never saw the light of day.

The editor's reasoning? Today's parents are extremely sensitive regarding their children's cognitive capabilities, with a considerable number in our school system involved in some sort of academic accommodation.

Whoops! This was a minefield I did not wish to step into. I agreed that the column should be quietly put to rest.

There are, of course, writers and comedians who still push the boundaries, but more often than not they do so on streaming services such as Netflix.

A good example is Ricky Gervais, best known as the creator of the hit TV show *The Office.*

His comedy specials are often profane romps through various cultural minefields, from the ever-growing array of pronouns and LGBTQ1A+ variants to the concept of "dead names."

He takes particular glee in sending up Caitlyn Jenner — so much so that you begin to suspect the two have made a secret pact to help keep her name in the public eye.

I do wonder what my uncle, a liberal in the classic sense of that word, would make of all this? Or his kindred spirit, Mel Brooks?

I am quite sure if Brooks tried to make something like *Blazing Saddles* today, much of the blaze would have to be extinguished.

And then I'd never have gotten to see my Uncle Neil rolling around in the aisle.

(Bob admits that he was so un-woke that when he first heard the expression "two-spirited" he thought the reference was to a cocktail.)

Lenny and the terrible, horrible, no good, very bad election

Image by Emmanuel Huybrechts under Creative Commons license

I almost feel sorry for Lenny Mirra.

For those who might have been holed up in a missile silo for the past nine weeks, Lenny Mirra, a Republican, lost a recount to represent Ipswich (among other towns) at the State House by one lone vote.

This came after leading his opponent, Democrat Kristin Kassner, by 10 votes in the initial tally.

Mirra is from Georgetown. Kassner is from Hamilton. And Ipswich, which had been in the Fourth District, ended up sandwiched between those two towns in a newly fashioned Second District after a recent redistricting. This remix had the effect of throwing two

Republicans, Rep. Brad Hill and Rep. Lenny Mirra, into the same electoral pot.

Brad Hill wisely decided to head for the hills; more specifically, to step aside and take up a plum position with the Massachusetts Gaming Commission. You might say he liked his odds better there.

This seemingly cleared the way for Mirra.

The only problem was that Mirra is a Republican.

Ipswich and adjacent towns had been reliably sending Republicans to the State House for more than 160 years. But that all ended in 2021, when Topsfield Democrat Jamie Belsito won the Fourth District seat vacated by Hill.

(Belsito was barred from running for the new Second District seat, as she resides outside its boundaries.)

Running as a Republican in 2022 Massachusetts was about as popular as standing for office as a Communist in Eastern Europe after the fall of the Berlin Wall.

Look at the numbers. All six of the state's top elective offices were won by Democrats. The entire federal delegation — our two Senate seats and nine House seats — are held by Democrats.

The State Senate has three Republicans, including our own senator, Minority Leader Bruce Tarr. They can't even form a bridge game.

The GOP House contingent is now down to 25 (out of 160) from 30 in 2020.

With the departure of Republican Governor Charlie Baker, Democrats will have achieved what is termed a "trifecta" — control of the governor's office plus both legislative houses.

Baker, consistently one of the most popular governors in the nation, decided not to seek a third term. And who can blame him? He would have faced a potentially brutal primary fight within his own party. Like Brad Hill, he decided there was life outside the elective arena.

So why do I almost feel sorry for Lenny Mirra? Because thanks to Massachusetts GOP State Committee Chair Jim Lyons and his merry band, Mirra, like all those running under the GOP banner, was burdened with an increasingly toxic brand.

You couldn't see it as he campaigned up and down the district, but Mirra was lugging around 245 pounds of Donald Trump.

Kristin Kassner, who by all accounts ran a good campaign, was not similarly burdened.

It would be easy to just write off the GOP altogether in the Bay State. But it is important to remember that Ronald Reagan won Massachusetts in back-to-back presidential contests in the 1980s. And the GOP has won the governorship numerous times since.

I congratulate Kristen Kassner for her win. And I pray the Massachusetts GOP can somehow untangle itself from Trumpism and re-emerge as a viable opposition party, one that can hold the majority party to account.

(Bob recalls the saying, "Power corrupts, and absolute power corrupts absolutely." He only recently discovered this was not a reference to the vodka.)

Five reasons why my running for Kristin Kassner's seat is a terrible idea

Massachusetts State House Chamber - Commonwealth of Massachusetts photo

A couple people recently urged me to run for the 2nd Essex State House seat currently held by Rep. Kristin Kassner (D-Hamilton). The idea, as they see it, is to win back a seat that was in Republican hands for more than 160 years.

There are lots of reasons why this is a terrible idea. Let me list them.

1. **I would have to live in the district.** Don't get me wrong – I would love to live in Ipswich, Hamilton, Rowley, Newbury, Georgetown (or in that silly sliver of Topsfield). But have you

looked at home prices or rentals lately? Most of my assets are in Canadian dollars, the Peso of the North. The only way to make this work would be for me to move back into my parent's basement at 15 South Village Green. And then somehow hope that the current owners, David & Jodi Quinn, don't notice or mind.

2. **My spouse would divorce me.** Karen likes Ipswich and the North Shore. But she hates politics. When we married decades ago, I had to sign a document giving her the power to have me forcibly committed to an insane asylum should I even think about returning to politics.
3. **Opposition researchers would have a field day.** I write a humor column. Among other things, I have playfully suggested that Ipswich High School dump their beloved tiger mascot for a clam or greenhead fly. I made a case for Hamilton to be absorbed back into Ipswich. I apologized to Rowley for decades of neglect. I admitted sneaking into the Topsfield Fair. These were all tongue-in-cheek. But presented by a crafty opponent, they would all look like foot-in-mouth.
4. **I would have to stop writing for Ipswich Local News.** The minute I declare candidacy, my column would be no more. While this probably wouldn't mean much to most people, its absence would leave fellow columnist Doug Brendel, whose work in this newspaper appears across the page from mine, feeling disoriented. Nobody wants a disoriented Doug!
5. **I would have to deal with Donald Trump.** I once described Donald Trump as a 245-pound burden that former Republican State Rep. Lenny Mirra had to carry around during his re-election bid. Judging from recent photographs, he now looks like a 275-pound burden – plus the weight of all those indictments.

Speaking of Donald Trump (and Joe Biden, Diane Feinstein, and Mitch McConnell), I would be 75 when I took office.

The last thing America needs is another politician well beyond their Best-By date.

When I worked in the U.S. Senate in the late 70's and early 80's, it was common knowledge that at least two senators were cognitively impaired. They were both southern Democrats. But in a spirit of bipartisanship, a few years later I was told by those in the know that Republican Senator Strom Thurmond should be added to that list.

Then there is the example of Ronald Reagan. We now know that the 40th President of the United States was likely experiencing the onset of Alzheimer's during his second term. This resulted in memory loss (real memory loss – not just ones of convenience when topics like Iran-Contra came up).

As far as I can tell, my cognitive abilities are currently intact. But who can say what tomorrow will bring?

If I did run for office (and somehow avoided my wife's edict to be placed in an insane asylum), the first thing I would do would be to propose an age cutoff for elected politicians.

Massachusetts already forces judges to retire at 70. And in Canada, Supreme Court Justices step down at 75.

When it comes to Bay State politicians, 75 sounds perfect to me.

I could then leave office after serving only one term. That would have the added benefit of allowing me to vacate my old room before the Quinn's discovered what those strange noises emanating from their basement had been.

(Bob wonders if serving in the Massachusetts legislature would meet his wife's edict that he be committed to an asylum?)

Striking out at Crane Beach

Steve McQueen and Faye Dunaway on location for the making of "The Thomas Crown Affair" on Crane Beach in 1968 (publicity photo)

We all know about the tragic Ipswich Mill strike of 1913, when police fired to break up a gathering of immigrant workers demanding increased wages. An innocent bystander, Nicoletta Papadopoulou, was fatally shot.

This is not that story.

Much as Shakespeare had his tragedies and comedies, this Ipswich labor story is something more akin the latter. Some might even call it farce.

The year was 1969. Crane Beach was in transition. Charlie Pickard, the much-loved beach manager, was being shunted aside by the not-for-profit Trustees of Reservations, who control both the beach and the adjacent Castle Hill property.

Charlie — we all called him Charlie — was a local Ipswich boy. Although "boy" might be a bit of a stretch, as he was in his 60s when I first started as a member of the Crane Crew in 1967.

The Crew was ably led by Sid Baer — today, Dr. Sid Baer — and at various times included folks such as Carl Nelson, Mike McSweeney, John Sullivan, Mike Chouinard, Charlie Mansfield, and Arthur Baer, among others.

The Crane Beach summer community also featured Bill Cruickshank, his partner, Joan, and Jill and Jan Pickard minding the beach store; and a slew of lifeguards — including this buoyant bunch: Robin Carter, Richard Haasnoot, Eric Melanson, Chuck Cooper, Norm Chambers, Howie Naugle, Jim Forrester, and Neil Cleary — led by Ken Spellman.

Beach security was overseen by, among others, Bobby Chambers and Charlie Surpitski (yes, *that* Charlie Surpitski).

As a 2023 reader, you might by now be noticing that this was something of a boy's club. No women lifeguards. No women on the crew. Guilty as charged.

But while that should have been something we noticed and gotten riled up about, it was not.

What got us going in 1969 was the manner of Charlie's departure… and the demeanor of his replacement, Col. Charles Coates.

Col. Coates was a West Point grad. He had commanded troops in the Pacific Theater. Retired, he now took charge of us on the Atlantic front.

Whereas Charlie had been something of a benevolent father figure, easy with a grin, Col. Coates was all business and grimace. He barked orders and was not above putting 17-year-olds in their place.

When a group of us complained about this to Charlie, he said, "Boys, life is too short to be mean." We understood he did not approve but was helpless to do anything about it.

Col. Coates seemed determined to whip us into shape, ignoring the fact that we were already working six days a week with a wage just above the then-minimum of $1.30 an hour with no overtime premium. This was at a time when inflation was over 5%, beginning its gallop to the hyperinflation of the '70s.

Finally, a group of us decided enough was enough. We met one evening in my family's South Green basement (a venue more suited to games of pool than plotting) and planned a strike action.

The next day, in the garage near the parking lot, we informed the Colonel that we would be withdrawing our services. The blue "please" trash barrels would go unemptied, the cars would park wherever their drivers pleased, the lawns at Castle Hill would go unmowed.

Col. Coates knew a mutiny when he saw one. "Anyone who does not go to work immediately will be fired."

We glanced around at each other (undoubtedly thinking about pending college tuition bills and such) and caved.

Leon Trotsky would have cringed, had he been there. Col. Coates just continued to grimace.

So ended the Glorious Crane Beach Strike of '69.

(The following summer Bob worked for Bill Wasserman's newspapers for $90 a week. On a per-hour basis, he actually made less. He says he never was much good at math.)

Dreaming of "Threesomes," Updike's unpublished sequel to "Couples"

Updike at play. Courtesy Golf Post.

I awoke from a feverish dream the other day. That's the thing about getting older — your dreams become more vivid even as your wakened senses grow duller.

In the dream, I discovered an unpublished John Updike manuscript titled *Threesomes* in his old office above the Choate Bridge Pub.

My excitement was palpable. Could this be the long-awaited sequel to *Couples*, Updike's 1968 novel chronicling the intertwining of 10 couples in a town called Tarbox? A town that bore a striking resemblance to Ipswich?

Couples also bore a passing resemblance to another New England-set potboiler, Grace Metalious' *Peyton Place*, which came out when

Mia Farrow was a pre-teen and Woody Allen was still funny. Except *Couples* was better written and more explicit.

Understand that the book's publication set our little town aflutter. Speculation as to who was who in the novel dominated conversations (and, in some cases, elicited nervous denials).

There were familiar settings, including my dad's dental office, which at that time was on the second floor of a Central Street office building. Indeed, Updike wrote the following in my dad's copy of the book: "To Dr. Robert Waite, without whom this ruthless expose of American dental practices would not have been possible." Thankfully, there was no reference to drilling.

The manuscript in my hand, no doubt created on Updike's electric Olympia 65c typewriter, looked to be in remarkable shape. There was nothing on the cover page except the title *Threesomes* and "John Updike." No date. No direction to his publishing house, Alfred A. Knopf, regarding font. Updike, like Steve Jobs, was notoriously fussy about font styles.

Who knew what plot twists and turns awaited? Would Freddy Thorne make a second appearance? Or the Hanamas, Piet and Angela? And would a fire at the old South Congregational Church on the South Green provide the climatic moment, much as the burning of the First Church did in the original? And might we learn, finally, who Foxy was?

My fingers trembled as I turned the page.

"Tom Marshfield could barely restrain a laugh," it began. "He and his two partners had executed their response perfectly. When Robert Coombes, the club's most officious member, had approached them inquiring about a game, Tom had replied curtly: 'Sorry. We already have a threesome.'"

I quickly realized what I had in my hands was not a furtherance of the Tarbox saga … but a book about golf!

And then I abruptly woke up.

I didn't even get to go downstairs to the pub to enjoy a heaping plate of fried clams and a cold one. Such are the wayward ways of dreams.

As I brushed my teeth that morning, I realized I must have been subconsciously channeling Updike's book *Golf Dreams* (or suffering the aftereffects of a second vodka tonic the night before).

Updike is best known for his writings about a fading high school basketball star, Rabbit Angstrom. And his best-loved sports essay, "Hub Fans Bid Kid Adieu," is a paean to Red Sox Hall-of-Famer Ted Williams.

But he had a real passion for golf.

I remember seeing him on off-season afternoons down at Crane's whacking balls repeatedly as he made his way down the beach. He was navigating the world's largest sand trap with the world's second-largest water hazard on one side.

People magazine, reviewing *Golf Dreams*, put it this way: "Hemingway had bullfights; Mailer, boxing. Updike has golf. He has long since established himself as the Jack Nicklaus of golf writing."

The *Philadelphia Inquirer* put it more succinctly: Updike's writing "lifts us from sand pit to rhapsody."

Updike once asserted that golf is neither work nor play, "but a trip."

And I'm determined to make another trip to that office above the Choate Bridge Pub to read more. And if the dream lasts long enough to enjoy some fried clams and a Sam Adams, so much the better.

"Tomorrow we will all be resurrected and play again."

— John Updike, *Golf Dreams*

(Bob and his two brothers play a round of golf each summer at a course, Shattuck, in New Hampshire. Instead of keeping score, they just tote up the number of lost balls.)

Ipswich would do well to avoid the townie vs. outsider vibe

Shortsonline

I think it might have been with sixth-grade teacher Francis Baumgartner that we read Shirley Jackson's riveting short story "The Lottery."

Published in 1948, the tale involves a small New England town and explores themes around insularity and resistance to change.

This popped into my mind as I read of the select board's "Townie Trifecta" elected last week. Comprising Linda Alexson, Michael Dougherty, and Charlie Surpitski, the trio — at least in the minds of their supporters — represent those who are deeply rooted in Ipswich.

As a self-styled townie myself, I am familiar with the sentiment. In reality, however, it is not even clear when one can legitimately claim to be a townie.

Growing up, my childhood friend Stephen Olech asserted you had to be born at Cable Hospital and live in Ipswich for at least two generations to be considered a true townie.

This revelation caused me to hide the fact that I was actually born in the Boston hospital where my mom worked as a nurse for fear that I would forever be considered an outsider.

What's worse, we had only been here for one generation, as my dad moved to Ipswich in 1949 to set up his dental practice.

I grew up with Charlie Surpitski and recall his dad, Stanley. Charlie is about as fine a person as you might ever want to encounter.

And while I don't personally know Linda or Michael, I assume they, too, are fine individuals. This column isn't about them.

It's about the danger in getting too caught up in the whole townie-versus-outsider vibe.

We saw a bit of this in the 2021 Boston mayoral election, when Boston native Annissa George tried to pin the outsider tag on Chicago-born Michelle Wu by asserting Wu was "not one of us."

George quickly backpedaled when commentators detected not only provincialism but more than a whiff of racism. Wu won with 64% of the vote.

My own observation over the years is that Ipswich fares best when there is a healthy infusion of new residents with new ideas balanced by those with long-standing town ties and experience.

I think back to my dad's time in town government in the 1950s and 1960s, first as chair of the school committee and then as finance committee chair.

Those committees had a mix of newcomers (including my dad) as well as folks deeply rooted in all things Ipswich.

And they got things done, including the introduction of special education programs, the cessation of corporal punishment (accomplished not without controversy, mind you) and the ending of double sessions at the junior and senior high schools.

Perhaps the best example involved sewerage treatment. Into the 1950s, the town had an open sewer — Farley's Brook — running through its downtown.

The Ipswich River was its final destination. Some of the locals seemed not to notice (or at least not notice enough to appropriate the millions needed to fix the problem).

Newcomers, with noses perhaps more sensitive to the stench, helped push through the needed bond issue.

We have just honored author John Updike with a plaque. In addition to writing some of his best fiction while in town, he also wrote a pageant for the town's 350th anniversary.

We sometimes forget that Updike was originally from Pennsylvania (much as some Pennsylvanians forget that Ben Franklin was originally from Boston).

And what would Ipswich journalism be without onetime newcomer Bill Wasserman? Or Ireland's gift to Ipswich, John Muldoon?

For those who might have been alarmed by my "Lottery" reference off the top, fear not. I do not see the good people of Ipswich busily creating piles of smooth stones in anticipation of an annual ritual whose origins are lost in the mists of time.

But I do think Ms. Baumgartner, one of this town's finest teachers, was trying to get us thinking outside our insular box when she assigned "The Lottery."

For me, at least, the lesson was to be skeptical of those who wish to do things as they've always been done.

And to be open to new ideas … even those emanating from people who are "from away."

(Bob notes that town historian Gordon Harris is from Mississippi… and that columnist Doug Brendel was found by Gordon while bobbing in a woven basket on that river.)

How watching the film "Plan 75" on my birthday made me paranoid

Publicity still from "Plan 75"

For my 74th birthday, my wife gave me a book on Malta and a ticket to see a movie.

The book was a travel guide to that history-rich country, one we plan to visit — along with Sicily — in the fall.

The movie ticket was to see a Japanese film, *Plan 75*.

I had never heard of it. Indeed, when I first read the title, I thought of "Freedom 55," an annuity program offered by a big insurance company that supposedly would allow you to retire, carefree, at age 55.

Well, I was wrong.

Directed by Chie Hayakawa, *Plan 75* depicts a near-future Japan where the elderly, upon turning 75, are offered voluntary euthanasia to deal with the strain of the country's aging population. The plan even offers a signing bonus and throws in free cremation.

Fresh-faced youths recruit their elders from strategically located kiosks. The end-of-life facility lobby looks like it was designed by the same firm that decks out Ritz-Carlton hotels. The intake personnel speak in soothing, valium-induced voices, reassuring entrants that all will be well. And that they can "opt out" at any point.

The director doesn't fully reveal how this program came to be implemented, but there are broad hints that the government outsourced activation of Plan 75 to the private sector. The government's motivation for all this? The very real fact that Japan has one of the lowest birthrates in the world. There are just not enough people entering the workforce to support the country's burgeoning senior cohort.

I found all of this unsettling. My spouse sensed this. "You didn't finish your popcorn," she said as the film's credits rolled. "Are you okay?"

"I'm fine," I responded with a forced smile. "I can't wait to see it adapted as a musical."

But on the ride home, I recalled I had just received a letter in the mail. It informed me that a life insurance policy that had been put in force by one of my former employers would be expiring when I turned 75.

The policy was ridiculously generous. But then, in a blink of an eye, it was scheduled to go to zero.

I had carelessly left the letter regarding policy's expiration out on a kitchen counter.

Soon after, I'm gifted a ticket to see *Plan 75*.

Coincidence? I think not.

The more I ruminate on this, the more the puzzle pieces begin to assemble.

For example, there is our trip to Sicily, championed by my partner. For anyone who watched the second season of *The White Lotus*, you know things did not end well in Sicily for one of the central characters.

And then there is the mysterious matter of Mike, who conducts cooking classes online. Mike's dishes are all vegan or vegetarian.

He uses exotic spices and other strange ingredients that I've never heard of. My spouse is a devotee of Mike's. We consume his recipes frequently. I fear death by kale and cilantro.

To combat the risk of poisoning, I had thought of enlisting our yellow lab, Kumi, as a food-taster. But the more I thought about it, the more I came to believe Kumi is in on the conspiracy.

How else to explain her habit of leaving her toys and gnarled beef bones on our stairs? Or her newfound penchant for licking my neck and ears while I am driving, nearly causing me to swerve into a ditch?

I explain all of this to my wife. She says I'm paranoid. But what's the old line? Just because you are paranoid doesn't mean they're not out to get you.

So if my columns mysteriously stop after June 17 next year, you'll know what happened. But don't bother looking for Karen or Kumi — they'll be on a beach in Sicily, sipping prosecco.

(Bob still doesn't know why one of his corporate employers insured him for so much, but suspects it was to keep him from ever returning.)

Disney copy-cats Adventureland and Pleasure Island flourished briefly

Public domain photo of Adventureland

In 1957, John Wyndham's science fiction classic *The Midwich Cuckoos* was published.

It tells the tale of an English village in which the women become pregnant by brood parasitic aliens.

That was certainly one way of explaining the post-war baby boom.

For Ipswich and other cities and towns across America, more conventional causes were cited.

But the fact remained: 1957 saw the birthrate peak at 4.3 million.

What entrepreneurs saw in this was a fast and growing market opportunity.

Ever ahead of the curve, Walt Disney opened his Disneyland theme park in Anaheim, Calif., in 1955. It was an immediate hit.

But for most Americans — and certainly for folks in Massachusetts — Disneyland was a faraway dream.

Flying a family of four or more to L.A. would have required a second mortgage.

Enter George Spalt.

The New York-based developer purchased 50 acres of land in Newbury and created "Adventureland."

While the region had amusement parks with rides and games in places like Salisbury and Hull's Nantasket Beach, Mr. Spalt was not above borrowing from the Disney model.

Public domain photo of Adventureland after it was closed

Opened in 1957, it featured "Storyland," which included the Old Woman in the Shoe (who, appropriate to the era, had "so many children she didn't know what to do"), Jack and the Beanstalk, Little Bo Peep, Jack and Jill, etc.

Park employees dressed in costume (including a baby bump for the Shoe lady).

Looming over everything at a height of 70 feet was a three-masted pirate ship complete with a Jolly Roger flag.

There was also a separate "Dodge City/Fort Apache"-themed section.

Set in a reedy area on the Newbury–Byfield line, it attempted to invoke the Wild West in the long-tamed East.

There were gunfights, bank robberies, and rides on a Wells Fargo stagecoach.

At Fort Apache, you were treated to inappropriate portrayals of indigenous peoples as savage "red men" who invariably lost out to the fort's U.S. Army defenders.

The park occasionally hosted local celebrities, including Rex Trailer and Big Brother Bob Emery (no relation to Orwell's Big Brother).

Families streamed to Adventureland from all over New England — upwards of 8,000 people per day during its first season.

Adventureland in its heyday (public domain)

Meanwhile, not far away, on the Lynnfield–Wakefield line, the designer of Disneyland, Corneluis Vanderbilt Wood, was carving up 80 acres to create "Pleasure Island."

(This is not to be confused with the Pleasure Island chain featuring adult "toys." It was the 1950s, after all.)

Opened on June 22, 1959, Pleasure Island was billed as the "Disneyland of the North."

It featured 48 rides, including the "Wreck of the Hesperus" (inspired by the Longfellow poem), an imposing King Neptune, and a huge animatronic Moby Dick that would rise from the deep and spout.

Memorably to those of a certain age, there was also a "Show Bowl" that hosted an ever-changing roster.

Everyone from crooner Ricky Nelson and *Bonanza* actor Michael Landon to Clayton Moore (TV's Lone Ranger) to the generational role-models the Three Stooges made an appearance.

There was also a pirate ride, the "Old Smokey" railroad line, a "Chisholm Trail" horseback trek, and — a personal favorite of our family — Hood's Gay Nineties Ice Cream Parlor.

The good times were not destined to last, however.

By 1963, Adventureland was on the auction block ... with no takers. In 1966, the pirate ship — which could be seen from the Scotland Road exit on I-95 — burned down. Fort Apache slowly sank back into the reeds.

And after (public domain)

For a number of years, in winter, you could still spy the crumbling concrete remains of what once had been the Old Woman's shoe.

Pleasure Island lasted a little longer. But with Walt Disney World under construction in Florida and scheduled to be opened in 1971, its owners threw in the towel, closing in 1969.

All that is left is Moby Dick, lurking at the bottom of a pond at the Edgewater Office Park.

Both parks ultimately blamed New England's short summers for their lack of success. I prefer to blame Walt Disney… on the theory that he was sired by space aliens in Midwich, England, with a mandate to conquer the world.

(Bob admits he loved going to Adventureland and Pleasure Island — and has since visited four Disney parks worldwide, proving it is indeed "A Small World After All.")

Award-winning Ipswich editor JD Curran wove a second act

Bob Waite (left) on his visit to see John Curran (courtesy photo)

LA MESA, Calif. — If there was a Parthenon dedicated to great Ipswich journalists, certainly Kitty Robertson and Bill Wasserman would be enshrined.

But to their names I would add another: John Curran, known as JD to friends and family.

For those under 50, you will likely not know of this individual. So let me introduce you to him.

For those over 50, let me recall a true friend to our town.

When Bill Wasserman bought the *Ipswich Chronicle* in 1961, he installed JD as editor.

He was young — barely 30. But then again, Bill Wasserman was young as well.

They were radically different in temperament. Bill could be mercurial; JD had an almost Zen-like ability to stay calm, no matter the chaos swirling around him.

In other words, they balanced one another.

That partnership saw the *Chronicle* rise to be the most-awarded weekly newspaper in New England, winning All-New England honors against far larger papers in 1969 and 1970 and sweeping Class 2 honors on at least seven other occasions in the 1960s and 70s.

JD was particularly successful as a photographer and in executing page design. He had an innate ability to orchestrate a photo in a way that gave it immediacy.

And his front pages, in particular, never failed to draw you in.

He was, in the best sense of the word, a craftsman: careful and meticulous.

When I first met JD in 1970, I was struck first by his resemblance to Abraham Lincoln. Tall and lanky, he sported a decidedly Lincolnesque beard and a wise and genial demeanor.

Whereas I was a bit intimidated by Bill, somebody who looked and sounded like Abraham Lincoln seemed immediately approachable.

JD in 17th century garb with his daughter's horse (courtesy photo)

Whether it was photography (where I only achieved modest success) or my page composition (which never approached his high standards), he was a patient teacher and mentor.

He also set an example regarding the power of investigative journalism. Alarmed by the clearly out-of-date property tax assessments in town, JD began to publish people's assessments each week.

Eventually, virtually everyone in Ipswich could see the inequalities, and a reassessment was ordered.

JD was also very much a part of Ipswich life. He and his wife, Bobbie, and their four children lived on Turkey Shore Road and took part in all manner of town activities, including 17th Century Day (later Olde Ipswich Days).

JD had a lifelong interest in textiles (his father had been the manager of a textile plant in Uxbridge) and could be seen out on the South Green working magic with his loom.

JD's stint at North Shore Weeklies came to an end in 1978, and, sadly, Bobbie passed some years afterwards.

I had an opportunity recently to spend some time with JD and his second wife, Nora, a former BBC journalist, at their home near San Diego.

Knowing he was 92 and in home hospice care, I was apprehensive.

I need not have been. Although somewhat frail, JD's mind was sharp, and he retained his wry sense of humor.

We talked of the sad decline of the Chronicle, and he expressed measured contempt for Gannett and the other companies ruthlessly gutting newsrooms.

He also expressed admiration for *Ipswich Local News* and the efforts of John Muldoon and the late Bill Wasserman to give the town the local journalism it deserves.

We, of course, discussed Bill. We agreed that despite his volatile nature, he made us better. And that having a rival paper for a period, *Ipswich Today*, had also spurred us to do better.

It has often been said that American lives lack second acts. That has certainly not been true for JD.

He stepped away from the *Chronicle*, but he quickly established himself as one of the Southwest's (if not America's) preeminent weavers.

Moving to New Mexico, his work was often exhibited and remains highly prized.

At the end of my visit, JD and Nora gave me a beautiful, hand-woven tapestry. It was perfect.

(Nora Curran has written an entertaining memoir, Tapestry of a Life, which, among other things, reveals that she and JD met on eHarmony. They married months afterwards in 2006.)

Fifty years ago, something wicked this way came

MCI-Norfolk (via Mass.gov)

Fifty years ago this coming week, sometime between 1 am and 3 a.m. on June 26, 1973, evil descended on our town.

Three lives were literally snuffed out, suffocated by the white plastic bags that had been fashioned into hoods and tightly taped around their necks.

The victims were Shirley Haas, 32; her son Gordon Jr., 4; and her daughter Melissa, 2. And there was an additional if less visible tragedy – Shirley was pregnant.

The murderer was Shirley's husband and the father of her children, Gordon Haas.

It was he who had purchased the items of their demise and brought these things to their Hodgkins Drive home.

It was also he who fashioned a sign reading, "(B)lack and white don't mix" and placed it in the master bedroom.

He also claimed he received a phone call at his Lechmere Sales office in Cambridge from "someone" expressing the same sentiment.

You need to understand that Shirley (Grant) Haas was African-American. And that her white husband was searching for a motive that pointed away from him.

All these years later it is difficult to convey just how traumatic the Haas murders were for those of us living in Ipswich.

People were shocked. There was widespread disbelief. And there was profound sorrow.

That trauma included two young investigating police officers, Charlie Surpitski and Arthur Solomonides.

Surpitski, now a select board member, recalls it as "one of the worst days of my life as a police officer.

The community was very upset – and somewhat fearful. Fortunately, solving the case quickly helped to allay those fears."

Officer Larry Jordan recalls being first on the scene the morning of the murder, followed closely by Solomonides. According to reporter Bill Castle, at the trial more than a year later Solomonides was still visibly shaken when he described to the court what he had observed. And who wouldn't have been?

The murders also received international attention.

I recall hearing from Ted Bergstrom, who was living at the time in Munich with his Ipswich-born wife, Priscilla Woleyko, that this was especially true in Germany, presumably because the murderer had a German surname – and many Germans still had deeply ingrained attitudes regarding race.

Normally with this type of anniversary story there would be an attempt by the writer to contact the perpetrator. Gordon Haas, now 79, sits in MCI-Norfolk, a medium security prison.

He likely would have told me he's earned a master's degree from BU while in prison. And that he advocates for prison hospice care.

But I have no interest in any of that.

This column is about the victims. And I don't just mean those that lost their lives, but also those who were tarred by Haas's cynical use of purported racism to throw authorities off the scent.

False flag racism is not new – just a few years earlier, in 1967, Charles Manson instructed his "family" to scrawl incendiary messages while committing the infamous Tate-LaBianca murders in LA. His intent was to incite a race war.

While it would be wrong to assert racism did not exist in 1973 Ipswich – it certainly did – I cannot recall a single instance of someone uttering a negative word about Shirley Haas. Quite the opposite.

Shirley headed up the town's surplus food program; she was president of the Ascension Memorial Church's nursery school; she had co-chaired the town's most recent Heart Fund Sweetheart Fair.

An article penned by Bill Wasserman just days after the murders, put it this way: "She was liked by everyone, loved by her friends, a warm vibrant woman whose life was devoted to helping her fellow man."

Shirley Haas was not a victim of racism, but of an equally insidious scourge, domestic violence. Indeed, Surpitski says it was "the epitome of domestic violence – it doesn't get any worse".

It seems Haas, who reportedly had an outside romantic interest on the go, apparently found his wife and their two children an inconvenience.

Murder is exceedingly rare in Ipswich. The next one did not take place for 30 years, with the killing of Tony Woo out on Route 1 in 2011.

Sadly, domestic violence continues to be prevalent virtually everywhere.

According to The National Center for Disease Control, 35.6% of women will experience physical violence by an intimate partner over a lifetime.

That statistic should give us all pause. And it is why we should not shy away from remembering Shirley Haas all these years later, as painful as the memory may be.

(Bob did not cover the trial, as he was by then residing out of state. But he admits that in any case he could not have equalled Bill Castle's incisive reporting.)

Following in the wake of Huck Finn on the mighty Ipswich River

Ipswich River - Courtesy photo

People ask if I purposely did stupid things when I was young, anticipating that it would eventually make good column material.

I find the question jarring. It is one I'm used to getting from family members, not complete strangers.

But it is true that doing dumb things can make for self-deprecatory humor. It is also true that I was very influenced by two of Mark Twain's literary characters: Tom Sawyer and Huck Finn, who so easily blundered into trouble.

Today you could be arrested by the literary thought police for reading *Huckleberry Finn* or *The Adventures of Tom Sawyer*.

But those novels were touchstones for many of my generation. Back then, being a boy was a license to engage in mischief.

Twain's Huck and Tom grew up in Hannibal, Missouri, on the banks of the mighty Mississippi. I grew up on the banks of the somewhat less mighty Ipswich River.

And while my friends and I were never able to fashion a serviceable raft Huck Finn-style, we did have an open cockpit two-person kayak.

It was a delicate craft, made of canvas stretched tightly over a wooden frame.

It had been gifted to my dad by the widow of his best friend, who had perished tragically in an air accident.

Not content to simply paddle around above the dam near my home or upriver to the railway bridge, a friend, David Holton, came up with the idea of launching far up the river, in Middleton, beyond Route 1 and the Topsfield Fairgrounds.

This was early April. The ice was just out, and the river swollen to near flood-stage from the seasonal melt.

The two of us convinced my mom to transport us very early on a Saturday morning to a spot where we could put in.

Let's just say that planning and logistics were not a hallmark of this expedition. We had no map.

Our provisions included two bottles of Coca-Cola and a couple of hot dogs. We did have matches, as we intended to eventually stop and build a fire.

The day was chilly and overcast with light rain.

After passing under the Route 1 bridge, we came to the fairgrounds — or what would have been the fairgrounds had they not been flooded, creating a kind of lake.

Fortunately, we were able to keep to the river, but finding the channel became a persistent challenge.

Indeed, at one point, we made a crucial mistake, continuing forward instead of veering to the left.

The channel became very straight… *too* straight, as it turned out. It eventually dawned on us that we were in a kind of canal.

Having lost a couple of hours, we retraced our route. (Years later, Wayne Castonguay, Watershed Association head, explained we had stumbled on the Salem-Beverly Canal, which siphons off water to slake the thirst of lawns and humans.)

By now wildly behind schedule, we found ourselves in a large meadow through which the river meandered, almost doubling back on itself in places.

Once past this, we found a spot to pull ashore, careful not to rip out the kayak's bottom on submerged branches or rocks.

We built a fire, cooked our hot dogs, and, shivering, heated the cola bottles — fortunately, only after removing the caps, thus averting death by shrapnel.

Back on the river, we paddled through a wildlife refuge and into Bradley Palmer Park. As twilight descended, we reached the Willowdale Dam and Foote's Canoe Rental.

At this point, we should have asked to use their phone to call home … but when you are 15, your brain does not work at a high level.

By the time we spied our destination behind the South Side cemetery, it was dark. Several individuals — including my mom and David's older brother — were frantically waving flashlights.

We were the Lost Boys of Ipswich (not to be confused with the Lost Boys of Hannibal, who disappeared in 1967 and have yet to be found).

I can honestly say my first thought on stepping ashore was not, "Gee, this will make a great column 60 years from now." It was "Gee, I really need a hot shower."

(Bob has since kayaked in places like Costa Rica, New Zealand, Patagonia, and Laos. He lets others do the planning.)

A modest proposal to solve all of Ipswich's planning problems

Let's hope the architect isn't having a bad day (Bing Create)

Let's face it: Ipswich is in a pickle. And not a sweet pickle, like a gherkin, but something more akin to a Van Holten Warhead — so sour it will require a week or more to unpucker.

Let's just review what's going on. First, there is the proposed public safety building. Singer-songwriter Jann Arden summed things up with a hit tune: "Unloved."

Some people don't like the location on Pine Swamp Road. Lots of people don't like the design, saying it doesn't fit in with the town's character.

A few people want to sneak into Essex on a moonless night and abscond with that town's public safety building, trading it for a structure to be named later.

Then there's the whole issue of Section 3A. the MBTA zoning law that requires density near train stations.

Specifically, it calls for zoning for 971 units in town, at least 40% of which are within half a mile of our Peatfield Street terminal.

And, of course, there's also the state's 40B low-income housing requirements.

Recently, a group of Harvard students from that school's Graduate School of Design took a look at Ipswich's downtown.

Not to besmirch their work, but it seems to me we deserve a second opinion. And where better to go than Yale?

This is a school that produced acclaimed architect Maya Lin, a bevy of Bushes, and Gary Trudeau and Brian Dowling. (I just won a $20 bet that I couldn't sneak the word "bevy" into this week's column.)

While the Harvard contingent played around with the town center, including the parking lot and the uncolor-coded Rubik's Cube that is 5 corners, I asked the Yalies to specifically tackle the MBTA and public safety building issues.

The faculty leader for the effort was Yale legacy-admit, Professor Prescott Bush VI. He and a dozen of his students looked at the issues confronting our fair town.

According to Professor Bush, it just took a trip to Pine Swamp Road, a bit of walking around the area in the vicinity of the train depot, and an end-of-tour stop at the Polish Legion of American Veterans (PLAV) watering hole to reach a conclusion.

"The state says they want intensification. The MBTA says they want density. The citizens of Ipswich want to preserve their open spaces but also want a colonial look. And the select board is worried about adding to the town's school burden and about water supply issues," Bush said.

"Our solution is to combine the public safety building with a 50-story tower located on the site of the PLAV."

I was incredulous (another 20 bucks won).

"The PLAV sits on a tiny lot," I said. "How are you going to wedge in a 50-story building? And what would it look like?"

"We'll take the surrounding lots by imminent domain," he said.

"Don't you mean 'eminent domain'?"

"When it comes to the state, eminent quickly becomes imminent," he countered.

He then went on to describe their solution in detail.

"The ground and second stories will house the police and fire departments. The façade will be so colonial that even Johnnie Winthrop, Jr., would be fooled," Bush chortled. "The third floor would house a reincarnation of the old K & G Bowling lanes. The next 46 stories would be apartments, with 20% of the 971 units reserved for those with low incomes."

"I'm no math genius," I interjected, "but that's only 49 floors. What about the 50th? And what about schooling all those kids?"

He smiled. "The 50th? That, of course, would be the new PLAV — part of the deal we'd strike. As for kids, our target audience is the elderly. Think about it: candlepin bowling, onsite police protection and EMS service, walking distance to the train, a rooftop tavern with a view of the Boston skyline. You'll see — seniors will flock in droves."

"Okay, but you haven't said anything about water. Water is a big issue in Ipswich."

Prof. Bush's brow momentarily furrowed. But then he brightened. "You are near the ocean, right? Just build a desalinization plant! With a colonial motif, of course!"

(Bob has already signed up for a unit on the 49th floor, so he can exercise by walking up one flight to the PLAV.)

Beguiled by dimples, pigtails, and a spunky sparkle in the eyes

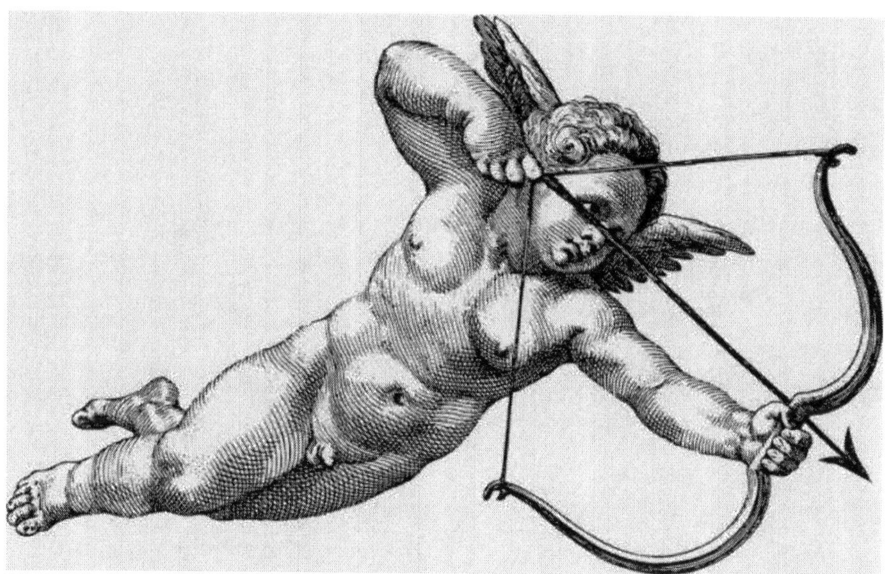

Public domain image

And they called it puppy love.
Oh, I guess they'll never know
How a young heart how it really feels
And why I love her so.

— Paul Anka, 1959

I was giving a friend a lift the other day. We had just concluded a school trustee meeting and dinner and were headed back to our hotel. This was Maine in winter after a snowfall, so I wasn't pressing the pedal to the floor.

Abruptly changing the subject from the school's business, I asked, "Do you recall your first crush?"

After a pause — one so long that I was becoming worried that he found the question as weird as it sounded to me as it left my mouth — he answered.

"Tammy. Her name was Tammy."

He went on to talk at length about Tammy, painting a word picture worthy of a script for a short film. Tammy was beguiling. Tammy even seemed momentarily attainable… until his older brother stepped in.

My own first crush involved an Ipswich girl I have known for so long that I cannot recall not knowing her. Her parents and mine were close friends, and visits between our households were frequent.

Like me, she was the oldest of her brood, and my age. She had dimples. Pigtails with bright ribbons. And a spunky sparkle in her eyes.

By the age of about five, I became hopelessly infatuated. This did not go unnoticed by her dad or mine, who sometimes teased in unison.

We marched through life in 1950s Ipswich somewhat in tandem. We both ended up taking dancing lessons from Shirley Tripp at the Memorial Building. We both went to Shatswell School, and we both eventually found ourselves in the "accelerated" stream (although neither of us ever really figured out exactly why).

That spunky sparkle later manifested itself on ski slopes, skating ponds, and on equestrian trails, where she appeared to me to be a fearless girl before there was a "Fearless Girl."

In a strange twist of fate, I was somehow cast opposite her in a play, *Father of the Year.* This must have been around sixth grade or so. I played the role of the father; she played my wife. This was long after the crush pangs had diminished. But when opening night came, I could not remember my lines — essentially as speechless on stage as I had been in her presence as a five-year-old.

Time passed. At Ipswich High School, I found myself having crushes on girls from upper grades (not exactly a winning strategy for a feckless freshman).

I eventually went off to an all-boys boarding school, where the closest you got to female companionship was a poster of Ursula Andress from the Bond film *Dr. No* on your dorm wall (or an occasional dance with an all-girls school, where they paired us off by height).

Decades passed. No longer constricted by height requirements, I married above my station and have two great kids. My only contact with my first crush came in the form of exchanges of condolences with the passing of our parents, a sad inevitability when you reach a certain age.

But it was memories of her that prompted me to ask my friend if he recalled his first crush. And, of course, he did. Don't we all?

(Bob refuses to name his first crush, but admits he later had a crush on a red 1970 Triumph Spitfire convertible in college.)

How I stamped out Osama bin Laden – and a woman in her birthday suit

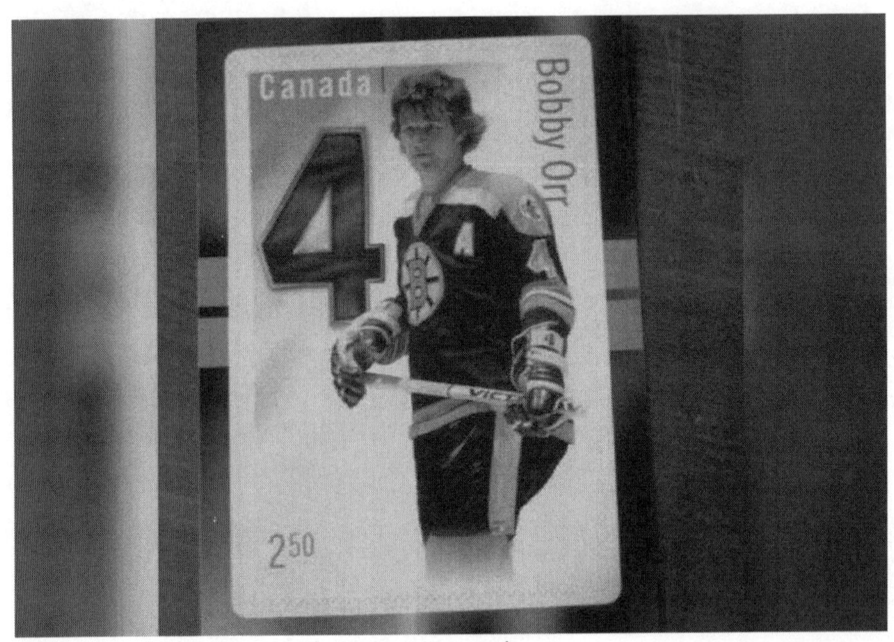

Processed By eBay with ImageMagick

As a kid, I used to collect stamps. I inherited my grandfather's stamp collection and decided to augment it with the latest U.S. issues. From time to time, I would wander to the post office on Market Street, stare for a moment at its wondrous Depression-era mural, and then buy a stamp or two for my Scott album.

This lasted about two years.

Flash-forward to 2005. I was a newly-named SVP at Canada Post Corporation. My boss, CEO Moya Greene, informed me that I was to chair the Stamp Advisory Committee, charged with selecting topics and designs for Canada's postage stamps.

The position had previously been held by the CEO. Moya, who is infinitely smarter than your average CEO, wanted nothing to do with being chair. "When someone is pestering me at a reception or meeting about who or what should go on a stamp," she told me, "I want to be able to point and say see that fellow over in the corner? Talk with him."

Like I said, she is smarter than your average CEO.

This is how a kid from Ipswich got to chair the committee that selects stamps for 40 million Canadians.

It is quite a leap from two years of collecting stamps to posing as a philatelist (look it up — it's not as bad as it sounds). But what made the transition relatively smooth was that I was given a free hand in reconstituting the committee, which was sclerotic. I also inherited an excellent and knowledgeable staff.

While on the committee, I pushed for greater diversity, instituted term limits, and declared that I would only vote if there was a tie. My only fudge was that I exempted myself from the term-limit rule — much like China's Xi Jinping, I extended my term (to a total of 14 years).

And we did some fun things, including coming up with a permanent stamp (before the U.S. introduced the Forever Stamp) and putting living people (other than the Queen) on stamps (again, prior to the U.S. doing so). Our first was jazz pianist Oscar Peterson.

And while I was never able to engineer a stamp for Ted Williams, we did get Bobby Orr onto one. And for a joint issue with the Americans, I made sure the map we used in the background showed Ipswich (if you had a magnifying glass).

But the most interesting facet of the job was something called Picture Post. The idea here was that you could send in a picture, and we'd create a real stamp (actually, a minimum of 50 stamps) using the image. We charged twice the face value for the service.

This proved popular with couples planning weddings — they would request a stamp depicting them to use for wedding invitations.

Another popular request was to put a pet — be it dog, cat, parrot, or python — on a stamp.

Of course, humans being what they are, we also got requests that fell outside the bounds of what Canada Post felt proper. And if there was any question, the image was sent to me.

Most of the decisions were pretty obvious. For example, on one occasion we received an image of Osama bin Laden. That was a hard no. Same with photos of a couple of members of the Tamil Tigers terrorist group from Sri Lanka.

But the strangest one to reach my desk was a photo sent in by an artist from Alberta featuring a woman in her birthday suit. And not just any woman, but the artist's spouse. After careful study, I rejected it.

The artist tried again, this time strategically placing three tiny maple leaves. I laughed ... but rejected that one as well.

That is what you get when you name a New Englander descended from Puritans to head up a Stamp Advisory Committee.

But I do wonder if I would have quit stamp-collecting quite so quickly had I been able to add such a stamp from the Ipswich Post Office to my Scott album.

(Bob was tempted to ask the artist to turn over a new leaf — but thought better of it.)

At the Riverview, pizza is an enduring family affair

Robert Waite photo

The HBO series *Succession* is about family members fighting tooth and nail over who takes over the business from the patriarch. This column is not about that.

Indeed, it is about a smooth generational transition and three siblings working together to keep an iconic local restaurant, the Riverview, in the family.

I recently sat down with the oldest, Joe Suslak, to learn how the torch was passed … and how things have been going since.

Joe related how his dad, Bob Suslak, had purchased the pizza place from the late Richard "Chick" Benirowski, who passed away in 2022 at age 100. Chick and his wife, Toni, had founded the restaurant in 1947, originally as a "spaghetti and meatball place" but fully focused on pizza (and drinks) by 1949.

"Dad was from Lynn," Joe recalled. "He had helped a co-worker who lived in Ipswich, Charlie Wilcox, move a stove. Charlie took him to the Riverview as a thank-you. Dad loved the place so much he left his number with the bartender, Priscilla, and said he would buy the place if it ever came up for sale."

A year later, in 1985, the deal was done. The only radical change made was the addition of broccoli as a topping; otherwise, the menu remained resolutely the same.

For the three Suslak children — Joe, Danielle, and James — the restaurant was the center of their lives. But as so often happens, each eventually moved away. Joe headed to New York and became a video editor. Danielle went away to school and became a teacher. James also moved to New York.

By 2017, after more than 30 years at the helm, the elder Suslak decided it was time to throw in the apron. It was at this point, according to Joe, that he and his siblings had to face the possibility that a place near and dear to their hearts (and stomachs) might pass out of the family.

Joe took the lead, but his sister and brother soon followed, drawn back to Ipswich by a common purpose.

For many, the idea of partnering with siblings is a frightening one. But not for this family.

"If anything, it has brought us closer together. We have a shared love of this place," he told me as we sat across from each other in a back-of-restaurant booth. "Plus," he said with a smile, "It helps there are three of us — it avoids tie votes."

Joe added, again with a smile, "We used to only see one another on vacations. Now, we see so much of each other, we take separate vacations!"

Joe admits that nostalgia is a huge drawing card for the restaurant. "Customers tell us this is the first place they come to when returning to Ipswich. We even get people coming all the way from Maine and New Hampshire wanting to experience what we offer."

It also probably helps that they have wait staff like Jean Flaherty, who has been on the job for 44 years.

When I asked about COVID, Joe says it was tough, but they got through it "better than most." They did a robust take-out business and — in a big shift — accepted credit cards for the first time.

For me, stepping into the Riverview on Estes Street, in a neighborhood affectionately known by locals as "Pole Alley," opens a portal to the past. From the jukebox to the pinewood paneling to the cozy booths and bright-vermilion barstools, you'd swear it was 1977. Or 1967. Or 1957.

When I spoke at the Lyceum in August, an old friend asked if I had eaten. I admitted I had not. "Well, the Riverview is still open," she offered. "Perfect!" was my retort.

I have a theory that the kind of pizza people like is the kind they started with. Deep-dish, thin crust, stuffed crust, Chicago-style, New York style, Greek — it is all a matter of taste and place.

Marcel Proust may have found remembrances of things past by dunking a madeleine in his lime-blossom tea, but for many of us, biting into a slice of pizza can have the same effect. Make mine kielbasa — and hold the broccoli!

(Bob recalls being in a corporate jet that landed mid-route because the CEO so liked a pizza from his college days that he ordered it to land to fetch one.)

How an Ipswich connection and a Rolling Stone Christmas party saved my career

'Tis the season of graduations. And of advice, sought and unsought.

I recently presided over a high school commencement. As a trustee, I was there to shake hands, smile, and utter words of encouragement to graduates as they crossed the stage.

Mercifully for me and for them, I did not have to address the assembled throng.

My students at Seneca College are not so fortunate. At the end of their year-long graduate program, with commencement looming, I deliver a "getting a job" lecture.

I can say, with something approaching modesty, that I am an expert at getting a job. I did so approximately a dozen times over the course of my career.

But the instructive story I tell my students involves a time when finding one proved challenging.

My partner at the time had received a post-grad fellowship to study at UC-Berkeley. We had been living in Nashville, where she was pursuing graduate studies at Vanderbilt.

I had a job with the Tennessee Department of Public Health as part of their communications team.

Life was good. I even got to play on the Vandy grad school softball team, hitting above my weight for the first time since Ipswich Little League.

But the move to California in 1975 did not go as smoothly. We chose to live in San Francisco. The city's two dailies, the *Examiner*, and the *Chronicle*, were not hiring.

I did manage to get a few freelance assignments from the *Bay Area Guardian*, the West Coast equivalent of the *Boston Phoenix*. But freelance failed to put bread on the table.

The person who got me in the door of the *Guardian* was a former *Ipswich Chronicle* reporter, Diarmuid McGuire, who had moved to the West Coast prior to my having done so.

"D", as we called him, was emblematic of a steady stream of bright young journalists that Bill Wasserman managed to lure to his North Shore Weeklies chain of papers.

He was a Princeton and Stanford grad, he had served in the Peace Corps in Uganda, and he was politically active, which suited Bill.

But, most importantly, he was a good colleague and took friendships seriously.

By December, after sending out countless résumés, I was utterly discouraged. While I would not have thought so at the time, I was edging into depression. It reached the point where I was reluctant to even go out – Brian Wilson Syndrome.

It was at that darkest moment that D called.

"I've got an invitation to a Christmas party, " he said. "It's at Jann Wenner's house. Why don't you tag along with me?"

Wenner was the publisher of *Rolling Stone* magazine. D had penned some articles for them. His going to the party made sense. My going did not.

"D, I don't really feel like going out to a party where I will only know you. I'll take a pass."

D would have none of it. "You're coming!" So I went.

The party was high-energy, which picked up my spirits.

I met interesting people and had interesting conversations about music, politics, and sports. (Yes, even the counter-culture retained an interest in sports.)

At one point, I went to the kitchen to refresh my beverage. There, I met a woman and got to talking. After about 20 minutes, she exclaimed, "I'm Sandy Close, head of Pacific News Service. Come to our offices on Monday. If you sound half as good when I'm sober, I'm going to hire you."

Which she did. And while PNS never paid well, I went on to cover the 1976 presidential primaries and eventually became the news agency's East European correspondent, based in Warsaw.

This was all thanks to D McGuire cajoling me to get out there one more time. Hence, my message to my new grads: Don't be afraid to use your contacts. And no matter how discouraged you might be, get out there and be visible … because you never know whom you might bump into in the kitchen.

(Sadly, Diarmuid McGuire passed away this spring. Bob remembers him for his infectious optimism… and for his beautiful, blue-eyed Siberian husky which, in Ipswich, followed him wherever he went.)

Ending seven decades of unfounded prejudice, I offer Rowley an apology

I have to be honest. I was taken completely by surprise by John Muldoon's decision to invade Rowley.

Sure, I knew the *Ipswich Local News* had some Rowley advertisers — notably, two cannabis purveyors, Fine Fettle and Cape Ann, as well as a popular dining spot, American BBQ.

I also knew John was a member of the Ipswich-Rowley Rotary Club , which meets at Rowley's Village Pancake House.

But I didn't think that restaurant's easygoing ambiance and location on the Ipswich-Rowley border would tempt him to move northwards to conquer the entire town.

But conquer he did. Aided by the U.S. Postal Service — and in a manner worthy of German military planner Alfred von Schlieffen — on the appointed day, every Rowley household received a copy of *Ipswich Local News.*

Why, you may ask, was I surprised by all this?

I'm ashamed to say that it comes down to generational prejudice.

Growing up, we Ipswich kids tended to look down on Rowley. We thought ourselves more sophisticated and worldly.

This was perhaps meant to compensate for the fact that Hamilton and Wenham kids often looked down on us. We needed our own object of superiority.

Sure, Rowley had a ski hill and a great diner, Agawam, out on Route 1. But the ski hill really wasn't much.

As for the diner, we lived in the belief that it had been stolen from downtown Ipswich one moonless night and surreptitiously moved.

Rowley also lacked a movie theater. We had the Strand.

And it also lacked train service.

My own father, as Ipswich School Committee chair, turned down an opportunity to join with Rowley to create what became Triton Regional High School (this, after being turned down by Hamilton).

In truth, as youths in those days, our attention was drawn to places south and west of town.

There was the allure of the North Shore Shopping Center in Peabody and, some years later, Liberty Tree Mall in Danvers.

A seminal event in our young lives was the opening in 1963 of the North Shore's first McDonald's restaurant, on the Beverly side of the Salem-Beverly bridge.

Those golden arches were as alluring to us as the Emerald City skyline was to Dorothy. We begged our parents to take us to a place where we could devour 15-cent hamburgers, munch on french fries liberally sprinkled with sugar, and slurp milkshakes containing no milk.

In matters of romance, there was also a tendency to look southwards. I even got caught up in this mania at one point.

A fellow Ipswichite, Stephen Grimes, told me he had spied in Hamilton "the most beautiful girl in the world" and bet me $10 (the equivalent of 67 McDonald's hamburgers) that I couldn't get her to go to a prom.

Much to my amazement (and Steve's chagrin) the girl, Carol Torson, accepted. It turned out she was a recent arrival from Ohio and had no knowledge of Ipswich's inferiority complex.

All of this is to say, based on prior prejudices, I probably would have aimed *Local News* expansion to the south — first conquering Hamilton, then Wenham.

My hidden agenda? Convincing residents there to turn over the Salem-Beverly Water Canal, which runs through those towns, to the Ipswich River Watershed Association.

But I now see the error of my ways. When I drive around Rowley today, I see a nicely maintained historic town center. I see architecturally appropriate public safety buildings and schools.

There is also the Jewel Mill, which sits on the site of America's first fulling mill (built in 1643), thought to be the birthplace of the colonial textile industry.

And, out on Route 1, they have a McDonald's!

I see a town with about 2,000 households whose population in the last census jumped more than five percent, to 6,161 (at a time when Hamilton's was declining).

All of which is to say I owe the good people of Rowley a heartfelt apology. But I'd still like to see the Agawam Diner moved back to downtown Ipswich. In broad daylight.

(Bob notes, in case you're wondering, that a fulling mill renders wool into felt.)

How wandering into the wrong breakfast got me thinking about circumcision

I recently stayed overnight at the Union Club of Boston. I had been the speaker at one of the club's author dinners, and the prospect of driving back to Ipswich at a late hour didn't make a lot of sense.

My room was on the second floor. I was told when I checked in that breakfast would be served on the fifth floor.

Armed with this information, the next morning, I pushed the "up" button on the elevator. The door opened … to a nearly full cab.

This was something of a surprise, as the club did not have many overnight guests. Beckoned to step aboard, I did so, saying "five, please."

There was a slight titter. "We're all going to five," one fellow passenger said with a smile.

When I exited, I realized I was probably in the wrong place. There was a sign-in table, and name tags were neatly laid out.

The men — and it was all men — seemed to mostly know one another. The ambiance was friendly — perhaps a little too friendly for this reserved New Englander.

I prepared to return to the elevator, muttering, "This can't be right." It did not go unheard. A gentleman who had been in the cab with me said, "As long as you are here, please join us."

I hesitated ... but then agreed to do so, following a life-long pattern of letting curiosity — and the offer of a free meal — get the better of me.

What I had stumbled onto was a meeting of the "Thursday Men's Breakfast," or TMB. Founded in 1981, it meets weekly and attracts about 50 attendees.

There is always a speaker, often an academic from places such as Gordon-Conwell or Andover-Newton or a nationally noted minister.

My host introduced me as a visitor, which very much reminded me of how my dad had once done so at Ipswich Rotary Club meetings.

My new best friend said, "This is Bob Waite. He showed up here by mistake after spending the night at the club and is about to head to Maine for a Hebron Academy trustee meeting."

Which brought a "Welcome, Bob!" chorus from the crowd.

There were also announcements regarding opportunities to go out evenings to the nearby Boston Common to administer to the homeless and to join a group dedicated to "praying for the city of Boston."

I wondered if they might throw in a prayer for the town of Ipswich (but kept that to myself).

The speaker for this particular breakfast was the Rev. Mark Booker, senior pastor at Boston's Park Street Church.

He'd done his theological studies at Oxford University and had ministered in places as diverse as Jackson, Miss., and Washington, D.C.

His chosen scripture was Galatians 2: 1-10. Now, I must confess that, as a lapsed Catholic and a wavering agnostic, my grasp of the scriptures is tenuous at best.

As Rev. Booker began, I was just beginning to attack the breakfast quiche set before me with my knife and fork.

It was at that very moment, knife poised, that I learned that the topic of this particular scripture was circumcision.

I quietly put down my knife. Part of me thought that this was something better discussed at dinner after cocktails … if at all.

It turned out, however, that Rev. Booker's talk was engaging and enlightening.

He walked us through St. Paul's reasoning in urging doing away with the Jewish circumcision requirement, which opened up Christianity — then, at best, a fledging minor sect — to the wider, non-Jewish world.

As the breakfast drew to a close, despite my initial misgivings, I was glad to have stumbled into the Thursday Men's Breakfast.

Instead of dining alone, staring into my scrambled eggs seeking the meaning of life, I had enjoyed a stimulating talk.

To top it all off, as things wrapped up, Tommy Walsh, a Hebron hockey whiz from my era who hailed from Arlington, came up to say hello.

We talked about hockey and old friends. But not a word about circumcision.

(TMB is not affiliated with the Union Club but uses their premises.)

Dark secrets lurk beneath the County Street Bridge

One section of the County Street bridge in Ipswich

Due to "deficiencies," the County Street bridge now carries traffic in only one direction.

Located downriver from its older and more famous cousin, Choate, the stone span is being given something of a rest until engineers figure out what to do next.

I'm not sure what the underlying issue might be — let's not forget that the great Mother's Day Flood of 2006 damaged five of the town's bridges and that, at any rate, several are centuries old.

But what I do know is that the County Street bridge was on my route to and from school during my Shatswell and junior high days.

Because the river is tidal, there was always something to see as you peered down into its ever-changing waters. I would especially pause to look at the span's separate side-chute, which acted to accelerate the outflow once the tide had turned. I never did figure out its purpose.

There were also what looked like ruined footings of a previous bridge on the downriver side — but no evidence of a connecting road. Such were the mysteries of childhood.

But none of this is what piqued my interest when I saw the news that engineers might be poking around the old structure, including, presumably, plumbing its footings and foundation.

The truth is, there are long-forgotten secrets buried in the mud beneath that bridge — secrets better kept under wraps. Including one of my own.

This goes back to my junior high days. Back then, we boys all had to take shop class. The girls all took something called "home economics." Yes, I know that by today's standards, this seems ridiculous. It accounts for the fact that 93% of all males over 70 cannot sew a button (although, oddly, 97% of women over 70 can swing a hammer).

Our shop class took place in a building adjacent to the old high school/junior high on Green Street. The brick structure had previously served as a jail. Hence, we would often pronounce we were "going to jail" when we marched the 50 yards or so between the two buildings.

Our teacher, if my memory serves, was a Mr. Thompson. He was a glass-half-full, optimistic fellow. He was also quite inventive when it came to dreaming up projects for us to undertake. In this particular case, we were to create something called a "pump lamp."

This project combined carpentry with electricity. We were to construct a lamp base made with slats of wood, a wooden trough, and a pump with a handle that would operate the cord for turning the light off and on.

There was a lot of measuring, cutting with a hand jigsaw, sanding, staining, drilling a hole for the electrical wires to pass through, and final assembly.

All of this took several weeks. And something called skill.

Several of my classmates excelled, perhaps aided by the fact that their dads had woodworking shops in their basements.

We had a pool table and a game called "skittles" in our basement.

By about the third week, with one week to go, it became pretty clear my project was completely off the rails. I went to Mr. Thompson. Ever the optimist, he said he was sure it would all turn out well in the end.

It didn't.

The final product looked like something Salvador Dali had concocted after having a few too many at the Panther Club. The slats and base were uneven to the point that the whole edifice, including the lamp and lampshade, were in danger of toppling over.

This masterpiece was meant to be a Mother's Day present. Nothing says "I love you" to your mom quite like bringing home a creaking fire hazard. Thus, when I got to the County Street bridge, I decided to end its existence by tossing it off the downriver side, where it sank ingloriously to the bottom.

Where I hope it will remain for the next 60 years.

(Still needing a gift, Bob went to Quint's Drug Store and bought his mom a perfectly square box of Russell Stover chocolates. Years later, he told her the truth — and like any good mother, she said she would have loved and cherished the lamp no matter how awful it looked.)

Rainy days and Mother's Day always make me sad

I was never very good when it came to Mother's Day.

As I related in a previous column, when I was in junior high, I was instructed to make a lamp suitable as a Mother's Day gift. Mine was so ungainly that I threw it from the County Street bridge into the Ipswich River.

Running out of time, I substituted a box of Russell Stover chocolates from Quint's Drug Store — not exactly an inspired move.

Previous attempts were no better.

When I was 12, I bought her a framed picture of John F. Kennedy for Mother's Day, thinking she admired the 35th president. She did … but I sensed that even a box of chocolates would have been a better choice.

For a time, I thought Mother's Day was invented by Hallmark — or Russell Stover — as a money grab. In reality, it was the brainchild of one Anna Jarvis, who, in 1908, wanted to honor not only her recently deceased mom, but mothers everywhere.

A few years later, when she saw how commercialized things had become, she publicly stated she regretted having done so.

But Mother's Day (and Father's Day) persist, which raises a point: can we ever truly thank parents — especially mothers — for all they have done for us?

Indeed, can we ever fully understand them, given that for the first 20 or 30 years of their lives, we weren't around to know them?

I thought I knew my mother … until she passed away, when I realized I had only scratched the surface of her life.

Perhaps because I am the oldest, or that I have had some experience in such things, I am the designated obituary writer in the family.

There were things I did know before diving deeper. I knew she was Anna Rose Bergmann before she became Nancy, and before becoming Nancy Waite. I knew she was a U.S. Army nurse during WWII and was a lieutenant — outranking our dad, who was a mere sergeant.

And I knew that after shepherding six kids into school age, she returned to her profession — this time as a school nurse, working with Violet De Mille.

She continued on in various nursing roles, including working with the developmentally disabled, until she was 75.

From time to time, my mom spoke of her childhood: her time at Ursuline Academy and St. Louis University and, most especially, her time in the army. But I have to admit, I didn't listen very closely.

Worse still, I didn't ask questions. And once they are gone, it is very hard to ask your parents questions.

But I did do research for her obituary into her wartime experience … and found that it had been extraordinary.

She had been assigned to O'Reilly General Hospital in Springfield, Missouri. The 1,000-bed facility was created during WWII to provide long-term medical care for returning soldiers, many with terrible injuries such as severe burns.

The hospital began using new innovations in plastic surgery to help the burn victims. It became a primary provider of reconstructive surgery and physical therapy, and many of its practices became standard medical procedure after the war. The facility became known far and wide as "the hospital with a soul."

As I looked into all of this, some of my mother's stories about her time there resurfaced from the deeper recesses of memory.

I recalled that she once told me that in administering to literally hundreds of dying soldiers, at the very end, they all called out for their mothers. "Not for their girlfriends," she related. "Not for their fathers. But for their mothers."

On this Mother's Day, I remember my mom and wish I had known her better. And if you are lucky enough to still have your mom around, I'd urge you to find out what she was up to before you showed up to interrupt her life. It just might prove to be extraordinary.

(Bob once wrote an obituary for one of his brothers … who was well and alive. It was not appreciated.)

Everything Everywhere All At Once left me nowhere

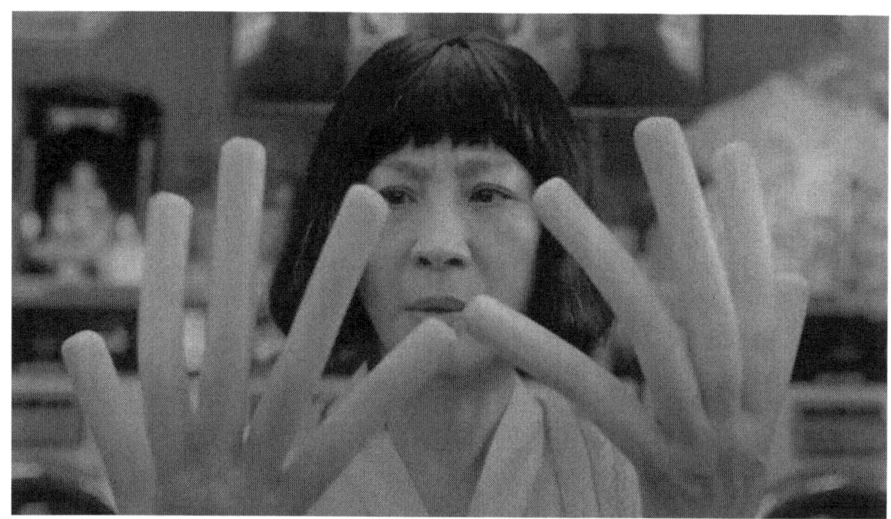

Michelle Yeoh in "Everything Everywhere All At Once" (courtesy)

With the Oscars rapidly approaching, I am still trying to fathom the film *Everything Everywhere All at Once*. Sure, it was nominated in 11 categories. And I get it that martial arts, the multiverse, and raccoons are currently all the rage.

Still, after watching it, I found myself confused beyond belief.

On the theory that three heads are better than one, I decided to convene a discussion panel of myself from three separate universes. To simplify things, I am Bob in this universe, Bobby in Universe 2, and Robert in 3.

We met to discuss the film in the janitor's closet at Ipswich Town Hall.

Bob: First of all, I want to thank all of us for meeting like this. And I apologize for the closet — the far nicer one at the Institution for Savings was fully booked.

Bobby: Let's get right to it. I'm assuming we all agree this film was about IRS overreach and the plight of immigrant small business, no?

Robert: That would be a hard no, Bobby. It's about the freedom to do anything because, to quote Freddie Mercury, nothing really matters at all.

Bob: But what about the raccoon? How does that fit the narrative?

Bobby: The raccoon was clearly an homage to *Ratatouille*, with a wink and a nod to *Guardians of the Galaxy*. By the way, Bob, why is my universe designated 2? Are you imposing hierarchy?

Bob: It was purely arbitrary, Bobby. Cool your jets. But as for homage, am I the only one who noticed the significance of the laundromat setting? Pure Stephen Frears from *My Beautiful Laundrette!* If you look closely in the background, you can see Daniel Day-Lewis unloading a dryer.

Robert: And what about Jamie Lee Curtis? Prosthetic device, or has she actually gained 40 pounds? Inquiring Universe 3 minds want to know.

Bobby: Forget Jamie Lee Curtis. The whole plot revolves around the yin-yang characters played by Stephanie Hsu. Her portrayal of Joy/Jobu Tupaki captured the essence of our dual nature — not to mention our universal attraction to large bagels.

Bob: I'm glad you brought that up. Am I the only one who saw the bagel as yet another antisemitic trope regarding control of the universe?

Robert and Bobby (in unison): Yep.

Bob: Okay, but what about that Oscar Meyer Weiner universe where people have hot dog fingers? All I could think about were frankfurter buns … and Dijon mustard.

Robert: I'm guessing you didn't *relish* that part. Sorry! Just a little Universe 3 humor.

Bobby: Very little! No wonder he designated you 3. But I did find it odd that two films nominated for best picture — *Everything* and *The Banshees of Inisherin* — were so, well, phalanges-obsessed.

Bob: I don't think we are getting anywhere regarding understanding this film. But as long as we are all here, just out of curiosity, what are your parallel lives like?

Bobby: I'm a meteorologist. Married my childhood sweetheart and have three kids — all named Bobby.

Bob: Hmm. And you, Robert?

Robert: Never married. Too scary. But I do own an African pygmy hedgehog. What about you, Bob?

Bob: I married an engineer and live an imaginary life in the town where I grew up, one infested with green-eyed vampires called greenheads.

Robert and Bobby (in unison): Yikes!

Bob: Just to wrap this up, should we have said anything about a spoiler alert off the top?

Bobby: Naw! The only picture anyone's going to actually see is *Top Gun: Maverick.*

(Bob admits his favorite film was an animated short, 'Marcel The Shell With Shoes On'.)

For reform-minded Fr. Verrill, Ipswich proved both a blessing and a curse

Public domain photo of Fr. Wendell Verrill

And when the radical priest
Come to get me released
We was all on the cover of Newsweek

— Paul Simon

Exactly 60 years ago this week, a newly minted priest, Father Oliver Wendell Verrill, arrived in Ipswich to take up his duties as the assistant at the old St. Joseph's Catholic Church up on Mount Pleasant Avenue.

These were times of great change. Pope John XXIII had convened a council — Vatican II — that enacted far-reaching reforms. Latin was largely replaced by the vernacular. Priests were flipped to the other side of the altar. Dialogue and cooperation with other faiths — ecumenicalism — was actively encouraged.

These changes were not without controversy … or opponents.

I recently caught up with Father V, as we kids called him. He's now 85 and lives in retirement in his native Hingham. I wanted to know what it was like coming into 1963-era Ipswich and where his career had taken him in the years since.

"I arrived in Ipswich two weeks after ordination by Cardinal Cushing in Boston," he recalled. "St. Joseph's was very simple, small, and was heated by a grill running down the middle of the aisle."

The church may have been heated, but he received a very chilly reception from the pastor, the Rev. William J. Melea.

"As was the case with many of my 45 Boston classmates, I immediately ran into an Old Guard pastor who strongly opposed Vatican II and all it stood for."

However, he recalls, "In Ipswich, I found kindred souls in the Rev. F. Goldthwaite "Goldy" Sherill of Ascension Memorial, Immanuel Baptist's Rev. Merle Pimentel, and Father Armond Provost at St. Stanislaus."

One issue they addressed collectively was civil rights, both nationally and here in town.

"A big deal at the time was a debate on whether minstrel shows in blackface should continue. I well remember that even one of the altar servers challenged my view that such entertainment is not appropriate. There were others objecting, but the show was eventually quietly shelved."

One of his great disappointments revolved around the historic civil rights march in Selma, Alabama.

"Rev. Sherrill organized a trip to Selma in support of the movement and, no doubt, to also make a point back home on what the Christian perspective should be. I wished to go but was told in no uncertain terms by Fr. Melea that my clerical responsibilities did not extend beyond the boundaries of our lovely town. I was to stay confined."

Soon afterwards, Father V found himself "exiled" to North Chelmsford — in his words, "as far away as they could send me from Boston." He again found himself tangling with his older superior — this time over the serving of wine at weddings. "There will be no chalice-drinking in this church," he was sternly told.

His career from there included missionary work in Bolivia (best known for tin mining and the end of the line for Butch Cassidy and the Sundance Kid), director at the Cushing Center for the Spanish Speaking in Boston, and pastor at bilingual St. Mary's in Waltham. An accomplished guitarist, he also made a name for himself as a member of the singing South Shore Men of Harmony and through numerous appearances on a Catholic TV program.

His final thoughts on his Ipswich stint? "I enjoyed the people and especially the teenagers of Ipswich," he says. And we teenagers felt the same way about him.

(Father V was one of the only priests to go on the record with the Boston Globe's Spotlight team criticizing the church's response to allegations of sexual impropriety.)

I felt the earth move – and it wasn't even my wedding night

Putting aside my wedding night, the most terrifying moment of my life occurred in Manila.

It was 1982, and I was on the top floor of the Philippine Plaza Hotel, which was built on land reclaimed from Manila Bay. Just as I was about to open the mini-bar, I heard a rumble.

Simultaneously, the building began to sway like a giant metronome. This went on for a good 50 seconds. My hotel survived, but the building next door pancaked, killing several people.

Needless to say, I returned to the mini-bar with a heightened sense of purpose.

Growing up in the northeastern quadrant of North America, I had never given much thought to earthquakes. That was something Californians needed to fret about.

As is so often the case, I was wrong.

A significant earthquake of about the same magnitude (6.0) as the one I experienced in Manila took place in New England in the early morning of November 18, 1755. And its epicenter was a mere 25 miles NNE of Ipswich.

According to T.F. Waters, writing in *Ipswich in the Massachusetts Bay Colony*, "Much damage was done to many houses." Similarly, R. Crowell of Essex wrote, "There was a great earthquake which threw down stone walls and the tops of many chimneys and bent the vanes on some of the steeples. It did much damage to many houses in this town."

So is the Great Cape Ann Earthquake of 1755 anything to worry about today?

According to the world's foremost authority on the topic, Boston College professor John E. Ebel, the answer is a qualified yes.

Dr. Ebel, a research scientist and former director of BC's Weston Observatory, told me, "The 1755 Cape Ann earthquake is a realistic scenario of what could happen in the future in the New England region and beyond, including in southeastern Canada."

In his book, *New England Earthquakes: The Surprising History of Seismic Activity in the Northeast*, he documents not only the 1755 quake but also a number of other damaging earthquakes (and a tsunami) that have affected the region in the past.

"There is definitely an earthquake hazard in the northeastern U.S.", said Dr. Ebel, "although that hazard is 30-100 times less than in California in any given year. Whereas they get damaging earthquakes every few years in California, New England gets a damaging earthquake every few hundred years."

Does that mean we are overdue? That is impossible to say with certainty. But a 2012 study involving modeling, including a scenario of a 5.8 magnitude earthquake with an epicenter in Newburyport, projected loss of life, injury to almost 500, and more than $3.7 billion in structural damage.

One reason the structural damage costs might be so high is that places like Boston's Back Bay are built on fill, which essentially turns to Jell-O when violently shaken. This happened to San Francisco's Marina District in the earthquake of 1989, when four died and a score of dwellings were destroyed.

Back in 1755, virtually all buildings in Ipswich were built of wood, which flexes far better than does brick or other types of masonry. It was the chimneys and rock walls that suffered much of the damage.

I went to Jeremiah Lewis, president of Bernard M. Sullivan Insurance, to find out if one can insure against this type of catastrophe. He had his sales manager, Rosie Anslono, do a bit of research. Here is what she produced:

"Earthquake is not automatically included in a homeowner policy and may only be purchased by adding the endorsement," she wrote. "The annual cost is approximately $175 based on a property with a replacement cost of $500,000."

She added, "There is a separate deductible for earthquake, and the lowest usually offered is 5% of the dwelling limit. This would equate to $25,000 based on a $500,000 property."

Like so many things in life, you "pays your money and you take your chances." Sort of like your wedding night.

(Bob was in a second earthquake (5.0) at his Ottawa dwelling in 2010. His family has never forgiven him for fleeing the house while forgetting the dog.)

When it comes to the 16-year-old vote, do girls rule and boys drool?

Back in 1968, the film *Wild In the Streets* featured a song called "Fourteen or Fight." The lyrics stated that 14-year-olds should be given the vote. (The film also featured comedian Richard Pryor as a rock band drummer, adding to its cult status).

Soon afterwards, the voting age was indeed lowered — from 21 to 18. Among the arguments for doing so amidst the backdrop of the Vietnam War was that if you were being sent to die for your country, you should at least be able to make your electoral preferences known.

Flash-forward to 2023. Ipswich is on the cusp of making a momentous enfranchisement move. Our town's 16-year-olds are to be given the vote, assuming town meeting attendees ratify the proposal.

As one who fought for and benefitted from the lowering of the voting age decades ago, you would expect me to be fully behind this change.

And you'd be half right.

Speaking as one who identifies as male and was once a teenage boy, I firmly believe that the voting age for girls should be lowered to 16. Boys? Leave it at 18. Or, given that the draft is now gone, perhaps raise it back to 21.

Science backs me up on this. Every study I've read says that boys take longer to mature in terms of social skills and the ability to exercise rational thought and judgment.

According to *Psychology Today*, scientists at Newcastle University in the U.K. have discovered that girls tend to optimize brain connections earlier than boys. The researchers conclude that this may explain why females generally mature faster in certain cognitive and emotional areas than males during childhood and adolescence.

On a personal level, I can attest to these findings in several ways. In my own case, a neutered three-year-old Boston terrier was capable of more rational decision-making than I was at 16. I could give you examples, but I will refrain (as I do not know the current statute of limitations laws).

Then there's our kids. Our daughter, Emily, had memorized the complete works of Shakespeare and was doing quadradic equations by the age of three. Our son, Joseph, on the other hand, was mostly bouncing soccer balls off his skull at 16 and thought *As You Like It* was just another way of saying "have it your way."

And why stop at the voting age?

Back in 1789, when our forefathers drew up the Constitution — and back when only men were allowed to vote or hold office —

it was stipulated that you needed to be 25 to be a member of the House of Representatives; 30 to be a senator; and 35 to be president.

Women were finally enfranchised in 1919 with the ratification of the 19th Amendment. But in retrospect, knowing now what we know regarding women's faster maturation, should the eligibility for federal office not have been lowered for them? Twenty-one for the House; twenty-five for the Senate; thirty for the presidency? Had they done so, Taylor Swift could already be planning for 2024 presidential primaries.

Which brings me to the other end of the age spectrum. Surely, the Founding Fathers did not anticipate a presidential race where an octogenarian would be squaring off with a septuagenarian. Even Ben Franklin, no spring chicken himself, would have thought it — in the immortal words of Vizzini in *The Princess Bride* — inconceivable.

Yet here we are. Joe Biden, at 80, wants to run again. Donald Trump, should he retake the White House, would be 77 on inauguration day. Does no one remember Ronald Reagan's second term, during which we experienced Iran-Contra — a convoluted attempt to arm Nicaraguan rebels — which the president said he failed to comprehend or even recall?

Perhaps we should institute a mandatory retirement age for politicians, like we do for airline pilots? Or some kind of test, as we do for drivers over 80? After all, a pilot can only do so much damage flying a 787. A doddering president steering the Ship of State could take us all down.

(Bob says he's against a mandatory retirement age for historians – he is still waiting for the final volume in 87-year-old Robert Caro's Lyndon Johnson biography series.)

Do destination weddings leave too many out in the cold?

After a two-year hiatus due to COVID, weddings are back with a vengeance. Venues such as the Great House at Castle Hill and the 1640 Hart House are heavily booked. As for getting to the church on time — or getting a church at all — planning well ahead has never been more important.

All of this came to mind recently while attending the wedding of my wife's cousin's daughter, a lovely affair held close to their home with all manner of family and friends in attendance.

Which brings me to the topic of "destination weddings."

For the uninitiated, destination weddings are ones that take place in exotic or picturesque locations, like on a hilltop in Tuscany, at the Four Seasons in Bali, or on a rocky outcropping in Antarctica.

A good example is Tiger Woods' marriage to Elin Nordegren at Sandy Lane in Barbados back in 2004. It cost a cool $3 million. And I am still waiting for my invitation.

If you haven't guessed by now, I am deeply skeptical regarding this mode of tying the knot. And I am not alone. According to various surveys, about half of us think they're great … while the other half think they are narcissistic, self-indulgent, and elitist.

Elitist because not everyone can afford an air ticket to Monte Carlo or Maui or a hotel room in Mauritius or Monterey.

Not surprisingly, the travel industry loves destination weddings, as do wedding planners (who get to tag along).

Here is an example from an Australian publication called *Cosmopolitan Event*:

"The only way your destination wedding would be selfish and rude is if you (the couple getting married) were being brats. By this, I mean that you are insisting that everyone attend regardless of their financial situation. If you're making guests feel bad for not being able to attend, then yes, you're selfish and rude by having a destination wedding!"

Basically, it is okay to leave out your financially strapped friends and family, as long as you don't taunt or shame them.

My skepticism regarding destination weddings goes back to having grown up in a relatively small town with close-knit ethnic enclaves. If you attended a Polish or Greek wedding in Ipswich, it was always a multi-generational, communal celebration. Sure, Uncle Thaddeus might get a bit out of hand or Aunt Sophia a tad too frisky, but the overall experience strengthened bonds.

There are, of course, arguments favoring destination weddings. Most of them come under the heading "Whose wedding is it, anyway?" And that is a fair question. In today's world, couples are much more likely to be in their 30s, rather than their early 20s. They are also more likely to be paying for things themselves, rather than having the bride's father foot the bill. And they may already be far from where they grew up. Their world is more likely to revolve primarily around friends rather than family. And if those friends have gobs of money, so much the better.

I get it. Being fabulous is fun.

This past week, for the first time in 34 years, my wife and I visited the venue for our wedding, the Enoch Turner Schoolhouse in Toronto. It is the oldest schoolhouse in the city; our guests actually sat on wooden benches adjacent to ancient wooden desks for the ceremony. Next door was a bright, spacious hall where the reception was held.

It was convenient to my wife's vast Toronto family — she has 28 cousins — but not too distant for mine to come up from Massachusetts. And it was fun.

Our daughter is now engaged. And she and her intended are mulling over the what and where when it comes to a wedding. Being the grumpy old traditionalist that I am, I prod them to opt for family over fabulous.

Unless, of course, the destination is Castle Hill or the Hart House. Then I'm all in.

(Bob Waite was married in a Buddhist ceremony and the reception featured New England and Japanese cuisine, including a Boston cream pie wedding cake.)

America from coast to coast is getting overstuffed with stuff

SANTA MONICA, Calif. — Beginning in the mid-1970s, I've made a habit of crisscrossing America by car. Sure, a jet plane is faster, but you miss a great deal by flying over the "fly-over states."

That's because there's a lot of America between Massachusetts and California or Oregon.

And while one of my favorite musicians, Talking Heads frontman David Byrne, croons, "I wouldn't live there if you paid me" in his song "Big Country," many people do, in fact, live there.

My first sojourn across the continent took place in 1975.

I took a meandering route that included places like pre-*Breaking Bad* Albuquerque, Barstow, Anaheim (to visit my sister Martha, who was with Walt Disney Productions), and finally ending up atop Russian Hill in San Francisco.

More recently, in the 2010s, I have twice traversed the Great Divide in a Ford Fiesta, delivering it to — and returning it from — our student daughter in California.

In that instance, I stopped to see friends in places such as Grand Island, Nebraska, and Carbondale, Colorado.

And now, as I write this, I am back on the road. What sticks out this time around?

We Americans are increasingly addicted to stuff — to moving it, buying it, storing it.

There are two types of structures that conspicuously dot today's landscape virtually everywhere I go.

The first involves huge warehouses (many, but not all, owned by Amazon); the second, self-storage facilities. All of them stuffed with stuff.

The other big difference from 50 or even 10 years ago? The amount of stuff on the move, lugged by tractor-trailers or by the railroads.

There are more than four million semis operating on U.S. highways today. I am pretty sure I must have passed half of them … when they weren't laboriously trying to pass each other.

Rail traffic? While the tonnage hasn't increased greatly over the past decade or two, the length of the trains and what they are carrying has. Trains are longer.

Often much longer. Many transport shipping containers — more stuff, much of it from China.

Other rail cars, typically black and cylindrical, transport oil — sticky stuff from places like North Dakota and Alberta.

And what about all that self-storage? In the U.S. today, there are more than 50,000 such facilities with a combined storage space of 2.3 billion square feet.

Think about that: 2.3 billion square feet! You could stuff all of Rhode Island in there and still have room for Delaware and the Big Island of Hawai'i!

A lot of this storage growth has been fueled by Baby Boomers downsizing.

They delude themselves by thinking their children will want their vintage waterbeds or rattan furniture, not to mention Grandma's cut-glass crystal or Wedgwood china.

So they rent space in storage facilities. Or fill up their garages, literally leaving their vehicles out in the cold.

Meanwhile, most young people have virtually no hope of ever buying a detached home — and can barely afford the rent on their 600-square-foot studio apartment.

In truth, I am not completely guiltless here. In 2006, we bought a larger house, ignoring the reality that our two children would soon be heading off to university.

It did not take long for us to fill up the extra space … with stuff.

I know what you are thinking — I've gone all Dali Lama or Pope Francis on you, railing against materialism and consumerism.

Or maybe I've fallen under the spell of de-cluttering guru Marie Kondo.

Not really. But don't you ever wonder when enough is enough?

They say that the American consumer is keeping the economy afloat. In reality, he or she may just be drowning us in our own stuff.

(Bob and his long-suffering spousal unit had their kids pick out the stuff they will want. The rest goes to their yellow lab, Kumi.)

Ipswich has problems – but they are "first world" problems

Clayton, N.M. — I recently criss-crossed the continent, careening to and from Santa Monica to Ipswich (with a brief stopover in Ottawa).

I did so with my long-suffering spouse, Karen, and our still-puppyish yellow lab, Kumi.

The journey involved putting 7,333 miles on our 2017 vintage vehicle. And 7,333 on vintage me — because much like Charlton Heston and his trusty AR-15, you would have to pry my cold, dead fingers off the steering wheel to get me to relinquish the driver's seat.

But this column is not about my demented need to feel in control or my antiquated notions regarding gender roles.

It is about Ipswich. In particular, it is about how, despite all of its perceived "problems," the town is still a privileged place to live and work. It is simply a matter of comparison.

As mentioned in a previous column, during the 2010s, I twice traversed the Great Divide in a Ford Fiesta — delivering it to, and returning it from, our student daughter in California.

In those instances, I stopped to see friends in places like Grand Island, Nebraska, and Carbondale, Colorado.

Each time I did this, I noticed a greater divide than the Great Divide. It is between those on the coasts, in towns like Santa Monica or Ipswich, and places like Clayton, New Mexico, or Oacoma, South Dakota.

Let me use Clayton as an example. It has its charms, including a classic movie theater (the Luna) and a historic hotel (the Eklund).

What it lacks is opportunity. Its population peaked in 1950 at 3,515 and dropped a whopping 11% in the decade leading up to the 2020 census.

The good people of Clayton have expressed their discontent by voting twice for Donald Trump, including 78% of the population opting for the then-president in 2020. This in a state won by Joe Biden.

There are a lot of specific reasons for Clayton's decline. Ranching is no longer what it once was in terms of employment.

There is no air or rail passenger transport. The town is distant from a major college or university. It experiences periodic blinding dust storms (and did so while we were there).

There are a lot of Claytons across America. There are even some in Massachusetts. Take North Adams. In 1900, the city had a population of 24,200.

Today it is home to 12,961. (How it maintains its status as a city is something of a mystery.)

In the plus column, North Adams boasts the Massachusetts Museum of Contemporary Art (MASS MoCA), which attracts visitors.

But in many respects, it is a hollowed-out version of its former self. Much like Clayton.

Things could be worse. As you ramble around the west, you occasionally encounter ghost towns: once-thriving places that dried up and blew away when the gold, silver, lead — or civic ambition – petered out.

My point here is that Ipswich has, in comparison to many places, what is referred to as a "high-class" or "first-world" problem.

Our town has to grapple with managing growth rather than dealing with decline.

This needs to be done thoughtfully — hopefully, with a minimum of rancor. And outside opinions, like those recently delivered by students from Harvard's Graduate School of Design, should be welcomed.

Outside mandates, like those delivered by the state? They can be resisted, but not ignored.

Ipswich needs careful, measured growth, not rapid development, or it risks choking itself in traffic and/or dying of thirst.

That is the needle that needs to be threaded by our various town boards. The task is daunting, but it sure beats trying to resuscitate Clayton, New Mexico.

(Bob says Clayton reminded him of the town in the 1971 film The Last Picture Show — but minus Cybill Shepherd.)

At Google, the future of work – is play!

Bob's hoop dreams fall short at Google LA HQ – Emily Waite photo

Venice, CA – My future son-in-law, a penny-bright fellow named Danny, recently took us on a tour of his workplace.

Danny works for Google. I am not sure exactly what he does, but from all accounts he is very good at it. Prior to Google he was good at doing stuff for Amazon and, before that, did good things for a company called Square.

Danny's go-to Google office is in LA, not far from his place in Santa Monica. But he is also free to go to Google offices in Paris, New York, Toronto, or Boston. Or he can work from home.

But with Google, why would you camp out at home if you can work at the office?

To start with, you can have breakfast, lunch, or dinner there – for free. I tried the breakfast – it was, to use a technical term, yummy.

Wandering around the campus-like facility, one encounters a fully equipped fitness center; a game room with foosball and pool tables; and areas featuring expresso machines, cold beverages, and snacks.

There are meeting rooms named for musical groups or performers, like Brian Wilson, The Doors, and the Black-Eyed Peas.

Outside is a climbing wall, a place to shoot hoops, and a small, fenced doggie play area. Dogs are welcomed at Google (except in the dining area).

Also outdoors are a row of available surf boards (the beach is not far away). And across from the doggie enclosure is a gleaming aluminum-clad Airstream RV.

"You can book it for a meeting or to just have a quiet place to think," Danny explains.

There's also a rooftop terrace with an oversized chess set and a bar.

What I'm not seeing much of are people working.

"That's because it is Friday," he says. "Very few people come in on Fridays."

To my dinosaur eyes, what I see is a lot of real estate overhead, without visible productivity. But what do I know? Google is one of the largest and most profitable companies in the world, with a market capitalization of $1.6 trillion. This is only slightly less than Canada's entire GDP.

They say that Envy is number four among the Seven Deadly Sins, just after Lust, and just before Gluttony. Am I envious? Guilty as charged.

My first jobs in Ipswich was working as a busboy at the Marguery Restaurant. You had to punch in using a time clock. And you risked getting punched out if you didn't hustle to the owner's liking. The only perk came on the rare occasion that someone left their baked stuffed lobster untouched, in which case we set upon it like crazed jackals.

As an editor at North Shore Weeklies, our one perk was a Friday morning breakfast prepared by our redoubtable publisher, Bill Wasserman. He served up scrambled eggs – but he also turned you to burnt toast if your paper that week was not up to his high standards.

I did eventually come to be employed by a company, IBM, which in its day was a colossus akin to Google. IBM was so successful that the U.S. initiated a sweeping anti-trust action against it. In one instance I recall receiving a directive to pre-pay for services well into the following year, just so we could report lower profits.

Ten years later IBM, which had missed a major shift in the computing market, hit a financial wall. The company lost a billion dollars back when that was considered serious money.

I had the gut-wrenching experience of downsizing my department from 72 to 18. We sold a company country club. And we reduced our real estate footprint world-wide by about a third.

All of this spun through my mind as I took a shot at Google's outdoor basketball court. I missed the rim – a classic air ball.

"Hey, Danny, any chance you could get me a job at Google?", I called out. "I really need to work on my jumper!"

(Bob says Danny's impending marriage to his daughter is part of a multi-generational scheme to raise the Waite clan's average IQ above 100.)

Arthur Wesley Dow wows them in St. Pete

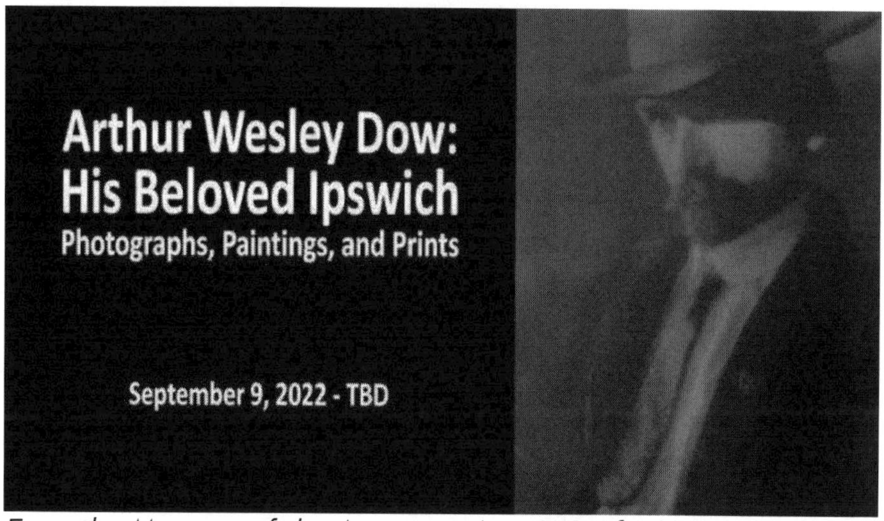

From the Museum of the American Arts & Crafts Movement

St. Petersburg, FL — When traveling, there's nothing quite like encountering a familiar hometown face.

I recently experienced that sense of surprise and delight when I ran into Ipswich artist Arthur Wesley Dow in St. Petersburg, Florida.

For someone who has been dead for 101 years, Dow looks remarkably vibrant. He and his works are on magnificent display at the Museum of the Arts and Crafts Movement (MAACM).

Call it serendipity, kismet, or plain dumb luck, but I had ended up at the doors of this museum due to a last-minute change in itinerary and on the advice of an old friend.

I had planned to be in Tarpon Springs; instead, due to my friend's unfortunate ill health, I ended up in downtown St. Pete.

Knowing nothing of this museum, which opened its doors on September 7, 2021, I was expecting to see displays of furniture, glassware, and pottery.

It has all of that, but the current centerpiece exhibit is "Arthur Wesley Dow: His Beloved Ipswich".

One of the cyanotypes with a view of the Ipswich River (via Museum of the American Arts & Crafts Movement www.museumaacm.org)

Housed in two large galleries on the fourth floor, it features over 60 works, including color woodblocks, paintings, and sketches.

Growing up in Ipswich, I had a passing acquaintance with the paintings and woodblock prints.

But what I found most interesting were original cyanotypes from his rare *Ipswich Days* album.

As a fellow townie, the 41 cyanotypes — a photographic process sensitive to the ultra-violet and blue light spectrum — revealed familiar settings in a different, almost spectral, light.

The exhibit is in many ways a love letter from Dow to Ipswich — most especially its river, marshes, shore-hugging structures, and countryside creeks and byways.

While fewer of his woodcuts and paintings are on display, the museum does an excellent job of tracing Dow's development as an artist, including his time honing his painting skills in France and the influence Japanese artists had on his woodblock printing technique.

The exhibit also highlights his influence as a teacher and mentor. Much of one of the galleries is devoted to his seminal 1899 book *Composition*, which influenced painters like Georgia O'Keeffe and remains in print to this day.

Another of Dow's photographs on Ipswich on display.

Museum-goers are invited to sit at an easel and, following Dow's instructions, sketch a rabbit.

My spouse did this well; I, on the other hand, handicapped by not taking Mark Hayes' art class at Ipswich High, passed on the opportunity.

It turns out the museum and its significant collection of Dow objects is the brainchild of Rudy Ciccarello, an Italian immigrant with Massachusetts connections.

He came to Boston as the commercial attaché at the Italian consulate, earned a degree at B.U. and a pharmacy degree at Northeastern, and went on to found Florida Infusion Services, delivering I.V. services to people in their homes.

Rudy's interest in the American Arts and Crafts movement — including Dow — prompted him to direct a sizable portion of his wealth to his Two Red Roses Foundation and to the museum.

He made his first Arts and Crafts purchase at an antiques auction in Boston in the late 90s. Things snowballed from there.

Flood Tide, Ipswich Marshes, 1917.

When interviewed by *St. Pete Catalyst*, an arts publication, regarding his interest in Dow, Ciccarello was effusive: "Dow's work is important because he codified the ideals and aesthetics of Japanese art and composition — not only in his own artistic practice, but also for teachers.

He had strong ideas about overall design that he explored throughout his lifetime. He changed the landscape of art and art education."

"Throughout our galleries at MAACM," he continued, "You can see the effect Dow had on the arts and artisans of the time, and the repercussions of his teaching are seen as a ripple throughout artistic production America for generations."

Not bad for an Ipswich boy. But at the end of my visit, I could not help but wonder what Dow would make of today's Ipswich, with its relentless march towards development and things like the pruning of the high school drama program.

At least his beloved marshes remain largely intact — much like his reputation.

(Bob bought the last copy of* Harmony of Reflected Light, *a collection of Dow's photographs, at the museum store. He has resisted placing it on eBay.)

Forget Chinese balloons and the Mexican border – fear the toothless beaver!

Adrian Raeside cartoon used with the cartoonist's permission.

Americans worry about Chinese balloons overhead and the border to the south, but maybe they should be more concerned about their neighbor to the north.

Canada — cute, cuddly Canada — is, in many respects, a national security risk. Not just to themselves, but to the United States as well.

During WWII, when British Prime Minister Winston Churchill and U.S. President Franklin Delano Roosevelt met to discuss wartime strategy, Churchill would inevitably call for an allied invasion of

Italy or the Balkans, striking at what he called "the soft underbelly of Europe."

Well, if you are a Chinese or Russian military strategist today, you might well think of Canada as the soft *overbelly* of North America.

When it comes to military procurement and preparedness, they are the gang who couldn't shoot straight. Or even find a gun to do so.

Let's start with military spending. Canada is a member of NATO. Member countries are meant to spend 2% of GDP on military preparedness. In 2021, the number was 1.32%. In dollar terms, Canada spends less than Australia, a country with only two-thirds of its population. This has been the case for decades.

Drill down, and things only get worse. The country's current number of "trained effective" regulars are just over 53,000, fully 20,000 below the government's target and the lowest in modern Canadian history. New England plus New York have more National Guard soldiers in uniform than does all of Canada's regular armed forces.

But even if Canada solved its staffing issues, there is the matter of equipment. Years of neglect have left Canada the equivalent of a toothless beaver.

Never has this been more evident than with Putin's brutal invasion of Ukraine. Canada speaks loudly — but carries a wet noodle. If the Canadian government's press releases were bullets, the Russians would be shaking in their boots. With great fanfare, Prime Minister Justin Trudeau announces what appears to be generous dollops of military aid.

But the reality is that this aid is either coming from already woefully depleted stocks or is being purchased from other countries — like the U.S. — who actually have the promised items.

A good example involves battle tanks. After a great deal of prodding, Canada announced it would provide Ukraine with Type 2 Leopards — a total of four. Ridiculed, they added four more. Why so few? Of the country's stock of 112, fully one-third are not fit for operation.

In late January, Canada announced it would provide Ukraine with a National Advanced Surface-to-Air Missile System (NASAMS). It then turned around and purchased it from the U.S., as it had none to offer.

This brings us to the thorny issue of procurement. Canada is terrible at buying stuff. I know this from first-hand experience at IBM and CAE, Inc. The latter company produces full-flight simulators and control systems.

Whether it is aircraft (like fighter jets or helicopters), ships (like frigates or submarines), air traffic control systems, or even a pay system for public servants, Public Service and Procurement Canada makes a mess of things. Canada's auditor general recently called the pay system procurement "an incomprehensible failure." Much could be said of a slew of others.

Part of the blame goes to the government of the day. When a new party comes to power, they often cancel whatever the previous government had in the pipeline. Trudeau cancelled his predecessor's order of F-35 jets in 2016 … only to reinstate the aircraft in 2023 after a costly re-bid process that will delay deployment until 2026 (at the earliest).

Until then, the country will fly its antique F-18s. Former Prime Minister Jean Chretien did much the same with helicopters in the 1990s.

This erosion of capability is a sad come-down for a country that fought valiantly at Vimy Ridge in World War I, on Juno Beach in WWII, and in Kandahar Province in Afghanistan two decades ago. Canada can — and should — do better. But content to nestle under the U.S. umbrella, it probably won't.

(Bob says the late Bill Wasserman told him he should occasionally write about Canada, as he circulates between Ottawa and Ipswich. He hopes after reading this column, Canada will still let him cross the border.)

On St. Patrick's Day, recalling growing up Irish in Ipswich

Dromoland Castle (hotel's website)

When I worked on Capitol Hill, there was one day a year when you wanted to listen to the Senate proceedings: St. Patrick's Day. And there was one senator you wanted to hear: Daniel Patrick Moynihan.

Moynihan in full flight on the topic of Ireland and Irishness had us all spellbound. Although a social scientist, on this day he was all about emotion.

As he once put it, "To be Irish is to know that, in the end, the world will break your heart."

At day's close, virtually everyone — regardless of party affiliation or ethnic background — adjourned to a Capitol Hill watering hole to hoist a Guinness or a Harp lager, the latter dyed green.

Bipartisanship at its best.

Despite my English surname and the fact that my Mom was of German ancestry, I was brought up Irish.

My Dad's mom was a Meany, and her mother was a Harty. We went to St. Joseph's, Ipswich's "Irish" parish.

Growing up, we were surrounded by families named Sullivan, Grimes, Hayes, Cleary, Downey, and Conley.

My youngest brother escaped being named Patrick by managing to be born on March 16. My youngest sister was named Patricia (after an Irish friend) and became known as Peggy, as in "Peg O' My Heart."

One of my earliest memories is of being rousted from bed by Dad, a Notre Dame alum, to watch *Knute Rockne, All American.*

Rockne was, of course, Norwegian, but that didn't stop Hollywood from casting Pat O'Brien in the lead role.

We endured more than our fair share of corned beef and cabbage. And Irish soda bread.

Some of this rubbed off. While I did not go to Notre Dame, I did enroll in an Irish literature course while at university in England.

The professor, Phillip Edwards, was a Shakespeare scholar, but his true passion was for the likes of Joyce, Yeats, Synge, and Shaw. I even ended up in Dublin to celebrate Joyce's Bloomsday.

And, of course, wherever I was on March 17 — be it Warsaw, New York, Toronto, or Ipswich — I found an opportunity to toast the venerable saint.

Memorable were Toronto's Ireland Fund events. Invited by my friend Terry Maguire, more than a thousand of us would lift our pints (and empty our wallets, giving to a group dedicated to peace and reconciliation).

My dad's love of all things Irish never waned, even as he did. He had been to Ireland once but longed to return.

Serendipity provided an opportunity. In June 1995, my two brothers and I were to be in the British and Irish Isles on business at the same time.

We connived with our employers to add on some time and arranged for Dad to join us.

Join us he did, flying into Shannon Airport in the west. We began what proved to be a fabulous eight-day sojourn at a place called Dromoland Castle.

Our itinerary called for a mix of golf, pubs, sightseeing, and genealogical sleuthing. We rented a Ford barely big enough for four (and barely small enough to navigate Ireland's narrow laneways).

Golfing involved we three boys playing while our Dad tagged along for the walk and the entertainment value of seeing his sons flail.

We played Lahinch, Ballybunion, Tralee, and Dromoland Castle's course. The goats at Lahinch could have played better than did we, but it was fun.

We went round the Ring of Kerry and the Dingle Peninsula. In Dingle proper, we had what our Dad proclaimed to his dying day to be the best oysters he'd ever tasted.

There was impromptu music in every village and food that went far beyond traditional pub fare.

Our weather was so perfect that after seven sunny days, the *Irish Times* warned of an impending drought.

On the eighth day it misted, but that didn't matter, as we were headed to the tiny village of Ballinvana in County Limerick to find traces of ancestors.

The local priest was gracious but could provide little help. He said whatever records hadn't been destroyed by Cromwell were burned during the Easter Rebellion. Sensing we might be hungry, he directed us to a pub.

The pub, it turned out, was packed and raucous. We quickly learned a wake was underway. Worried that we were intruding, we tried to leave.

The locals would have none of it. So that was our Irish send-off — sharing a pint with our new best friends at a wake for one newly departed. Daniel Patrick Moynahan would have loved it. My Dad certainly did.

(Senator Moynihan once famously said, "Everyone is entitled to his own opinion, but not his own facts.")

Trying to break the language barrier nearly broke me

Bob can only sit on one branch of this tree.

Ipswich High School once had a teacher by the name of David Welsh. Mr. Welsh taught French, Latin, and drivers' ed.

Short in stature, he was long on patience.

I know this — not because of drivers' ed. (I knew how to drive) — but from taking French with him.

You have to understand that foreign languages and I just do not get along.

For one thing they are so … well, *foreign*. If God had wanted me to speak French, He would have plopped me down in France or, at the very least, Quebec. And anyway, as near as I can figure, God speaks Hebrew and Latin (with a little Yiddish thrown in for comic relief).

It was with Latin that I had my first linguistic stumble. All my neighborhood buddies were becoming altar boys, which involved wearing a kind of dress or jumper — I think it was called a cassock — along with well-polished black shoes.

It also involved learning Latin. Or, in my case, *not* learning Latin.

Being drummed out of the altar boy corps was humiliating. You had to ceremoniously turn in your cassock. Worse still, you had to keep the shiny black shoes, whose only possible use would involve your own funeral.

Next came French and Mr. Welsh. To say I was a poor French student is like saying former Red Sox player Pablo "Panda" Sandoval was merely poor as a third baseman. Like the Panda, I was a train wreck.

Mr. Welsh did his best to try to encourage me to keep at it.

"Not everybody in the world speaks English," he would say. "Someday, you may go to Europe, perhaps even to France, and you'll regret not knowing the language."

I was unmoved by this well-meaning advice. After all, I'd been around. At age 12, I'd gone to Florida. And I'd also been to places like Amesbury and Tewksbury to watch Ipswich High football games. Not once did I need to *parlez-vous.*

Next, I tried German. By this time, I had been spirited off to the woods of Maine to attend a prep school, Hebron Academy. It seemed like a good time to chuck French and go Teutonic. After all, in movies Germans were always saying, "Ve have vays of making you talk." Maybe that included having ways to talk in German.

Again, despite the best effort of another infinitely patient teacher, Herr Jay Woolsey (who had been in military intelligence and probably *did* have ways to make people talk), I was again an utter failure.

An intervention was deemed in order. I was sent to the Holyoke Center at Harvard to be evaluated by a professor reputed to be the world's foremost expert on language acquisition. I spent an entire morning taking every conceivable test (plus a few that were inconceivable).

At the end of all that, the professor came out to meet with me. My parents were there as well. The man was positively beaming.

"All I can say," he enthused, "Is that you, young man, achieved the lowest score of anyone who has ever taken these tests. I am amazed you ever learned English. This is one for the journals."

The report exempted me from further foreign language study at Hebron. Years later, it exempted me from a requirement to be bilingual in a job. When asked if I spoke French, I answered "I'm from Boston — you're lucky I speak English!"

Ironically, I now teach a college graduate course called "international communications." In it, I stress the importance of learning languages. Yes, this is a classic case of do as I say, not as I do. Where was Google Translate when I really needed it?

(Bob believes both David Welsh and Jay Woolsey deserve sainthood for the hell he put them through.)

Autumn brings memories of Coach Roundy and football's seductive allure

Elliott Roundy

I love football.

Maybe not in the way Supreme Court Justice Brett Kavanaugh professes to love beer, but I'd be the first to admit that when September rolls around, my attention turns to the gridiron.

This goes back to my childhood. My dad, who attended Notre Dame, sat me down in front of our black-and-white Philco TV at the age of three to watch *Knute Rockne, All American.* The 1940 film featured an Irishman, Pat O'Brien, playing Norway-born Rockne, and some fellow named Ronald Reagan cast as a dying George Gipp.

Every autumn, the boys in our neighborhood would play football out on the South Green, with our errant passes sometimes bringing vehicles to a screeching halt on Route 1A. The Green was wider back then — certainly wider than our common sense.

One of the older members of our neighborhood gang, Shaun Hayes, eventually became the football team manager of the Ipswich High Tigers. Invoking the great powers invested in that office, he deputized several of us as his assistants. And not just any assistants — "water boys."

This was back in the '60s, long before Adam Sandler immortalized the job on film.

Being a water boy was great. It afforded us bench-side seats at every Tigers football game. These were the days of coach Elliott Roundy, without a doubt the most demonstrative and emotional figure I have ever encountered.

Given a choice between watching Coach Roundy on game day or Sir Laurence Olivier perform in *Hamlet*, I'd opt for coach Roundy every time.

Roundy had a unique way of conveying the life-and-death seriousness of the task at hand, employing facial expressions, a rapidly rising pitch of voice, and body language contortions that sent anyone within earshot into a frenzy. His players loved him — as did we mere water boys.

In those days, if memory serves, Ipswich mostly employed a now antiquated single-wing offense. Unlike today's pass-happy schemes, the main weapon was the run. And my favorite runner, by far, was a fellow named Paul "Monk" Sousa.

Possessing just the right combination of strength and speed, Sousa would at times pound through defenders, but more often would elude them by suddenly shifting into a higher gear. Sought after by colleges, he would eventually go on to Dalhousie University in Halifax, Nova Scotia.

When I first arrived in high school myself, I was too light to have any chance of making the football squad. Instead, I became a "harrier," a cross-country runner of middling ability. It was only when I was spirited off to Hebron Academy that I turned my attention to football. Eventually, I became the smallest (155 lbs) center and the slowest cornerback in northern New England prep history.

And while we did not have a Coach Roundy, we did have a head coach named Tom Ossman, a bowling ball of a man who still holds Harvard's rushing record of five touchdowns in a single game. Ossman was the anti-Roundy, seldom given to emotion of any kind.

At Hebron, I did experience what it can be like when 11 individuals "do their job" and move the team down the field. Perhaps more than any other sport, that ability to work in cohesive unison is key to success.

From there, it was on to the University of Wisconsin, where I became a Badger — and have lived and died with that school's football fortunes ever since.

At this point, I need to confess that football has become a decidedly guilty pleasure. And one that I cannot always easily defend. My spouse thinks the sport barbaric. My son opted for soccer — and I was not unhappy, given the growing evidence that football can cause cognitive issues.

As a professor, I even assign this essay topic: "Pro football is to the U.S. what the gladiatorial games were to Romans: Discuss."

But for all of that, I cannot help myself. It is autumn. My mind harkens back to the days of Coach Elliott Roundy. And looks ahead to games as yet unplayed.

(Bob admits he was concussed during one game — and in the film afterwards, he saw himself run into his own fullback, bringing him down better than he ever did any opponent.)

In today's world, can a good person be a great president?

Jimmy Carter in the Oval Office in 1978. (public domain)

Jimmy Carter, who recently entered hospice care, is the Herbert Hoover of American presidents.

Like Hoover, Carter is widely regarded to have been an exemplary individual genuinely dedicated to the pursuit of peace and the promotion of human rights.

Like Hoover, he is considered by many historians to be, if not a failed president, then one consigned to the mid-echelons, hanging out with the likes of William Taft and James Garfield in some rankings.

Which raises an interesting question: Can a good person be a successful president?

This is a question I asked myself when covering Jimmy Carter during the 1976 Wisconsin primary.

I was a correspondent for Pacific News Service (PNS). Wisconsin was a pivotable state in a wide-open race. Carter, at that point, was the front-runner … but a shaky one. Senator Henry "Scoop" Jackson of Washington had won Massachusetts; pundits had left-leaning Rep. Morris Udall of Arizona pegged to win in America's Dairyland.

Wisconsin was something of a homecoming for me — I had been a university student in Madison. One thing I had learned was that the state outside of that ultra-liberal bubble was quite different in political temperament.

I observed up close Carter's ability to connect with the state's farmers and Christian evangelicals. In my only one-on-one encounter, I was impressed by how quickly he formed a personal bond. He looked directly at you with those piercing hazel eyes of his and spoke so softly that you were forced to lean forward to catch every word.

I filed a story predicting he would be the nominee and would move the Democrats — who had suffered a historic defeat in 1972 by nominating George McGovern — to the center. Left unsaid were my fears that Carter, a former Georgia governor who seemed most comfortable teaching Sunday School in his hometown of Plains, might not be tough enough for the job.

By the time the November election rolled around, I was in Warsaw, Poland, serving as PNS' Eastern European correspondent. This was during the Cold War, and I was deep behind the Iron Curtain. The Soviet Union wasn't just close at hand — they were a military presence.

Voting absentee, I cast my ballot for President Ford, believing Carter to be untested and prone to naivety. Never a fan of Richard Nixon, it was the first time I had voted for a Republican presidential candidate. Carter, of course, won that election.

The next time I met Jimmy Carter was in the Oval Office. It was 1978, and I was by now Senator Edward Brooke's press secretary. A treaty to turn the Panama Canal over to Panamanians was the hot issue of the day. Brooke was insisting on amendments he believed strengthened U.S. strategic interests.

The Jimmy Carter I encountered that day was little different from the one I had met previously, with the same piercing eyes and soft voice. He was gracious and accommodating. Brooke got the assurances he desired, and the president got the treaty vote he needed.

Many people recall Carter's shortcomings as president — the Iranian hostage crisis, rising inflation and unemployment, his inability to keep his party united — but too often forget his accomplishments, which included not only the canal treaty but also the Camp David Accords and the establishment of a national energy policy.

His underlying problem, in my view, was his inability to project an optimistic future for America. His heart was in the right place, but his use of expressions like "national malaise" did not inspire confidence. He was doomed to fall to the eternally sunny Ronald Reagan.

His life after the presidency was exemplary. The Carter Center promoted democracy and peace. His efforts with Habitat for Humanity were legendary. He won a Nobel Peace Prize in 2002.

I mentioned Herbert Hoover. In the unlikely event you ever find yourself in West Branch, Iowa, visit the Hoover Library. You will see the same story — a good man with good intentions undone by bad luck and timing. One who then returned to doing good for the remainder of his life.

Shakespeare's Marc Antony said of Caesar, "The evil men do lives after them, while the good is oft interred with their bones." Jimmy Carter did no evil, and the good deserves to live after him.

(Bob admits he visits presidential libraries for fun ... and the Ipswich Library for research.)

At Bob Dole's 100th we recalled his humor and his urge to get things done

Lawrence, KS – My spouse and I went to a 100th birthday party recently. We were among about 300 in attendance. Unfortunately, the individual being honored wasn't able to make it.

Bob Dole, the former Senate Majority Leader, and Republican presidential nominee, missed crossing the century threshold by 18 months. Fighting Stage-4 cancer, he had known getting to 100 would be tough.

Interviewed by CBS's Rita Braver in 2021, he was the same Bob Dole I knew from my time with him as his press secretary — sharp of mind and ready with a quip.

When wife Elizabeth said she was planning for his 100th birthday, he deadpanned, "And I hope to be there." Sadly, it wasn't to be.

But those of us who did make it recalled Dole's wit; his many legislative achievements; and his simple advice to those aspiring to a life of service – Work Hard; Help Others; Always Remember Where You Come From.

Dole was from Russell, Kansas, a wind-swept western prairie town, population 4,401. He never forgot them and they never forgot him. Indeed, an impressive number made the 206-mile drive to Lawrence on I-70 to bear witness to all he had meant to them.

Equally impressive was the list of individuals who provided in-person or video greetings at the opening dinner, including former Secretary of State Condoleezza Rice, former Governor and HHS Secretary Kathleen Sebelius, and the man who defeated him in 1996, Bill Clinton. We were also blessed by the presence of the Senator's only child, daughter Robin.

The dinner's keynote speaker was another son of the Kansas plains, former Wall Street Journal DC Bureau Chief Gerald F. Seib. His talk "An Only in-America Story For our Times", stressed that Dole's great gift was to forge bipartisan alliances and "get things done."

Among those "things" was the rescue of a teetering social security system; passage of the Americans With Disabilities Act; an overhaul of the tax code; Martin Luther King Day; the establishment of a World War II monument on the Mall; and passage of a host of legislation benefitting veterans, farmers, women, and children.

Seib added that another salient Dole attribute was that "he could make a joke – and take a joke."

This theme continued throughout the two-day event.

Speakers recalled the time Dole was shown a picture of Presidents Carter, Ford and Nixon poised together. "See no evil; Hear no evil; and – Evil" was his instant quip, carried by media to the world. (As his former press secretary, I can attest to the fact that Bob Dole's ability to transmit his thoughts directly to his lips was unprecedented. In this case, he later quietly apologized to Nixon.)

But most of his humor was self-deprecatory. For example, when Dole lost the New Hampshire GOP primary in 1980, gathering only 607 votes, he was asked the next morning how he felt. "I slept like a baby," he deadpanned. "I woke up every two hours and cried."

One of the participants in the sessions the next day at the Dole Institute of Politics on the campus of the University of Kansas was a former colleague of mine from both the Ed Brooke and Bob Dole Senate staffs – Richard Norton Smith.

A native of Leominster, Smith is one of America's preeminent political biographers and has the distinction of having served as Director of no less than four Presidential Libraries. But of particular relevance to this event, he was the founding director of KU's Dole Institute.

Dedicated to fostering bipartisanship and civic engagement, the Institute was founded 20 years ago by Bob and Elizabeth Dole. It brings together individuals from across the political spectrum.

When asked to name one of Bob Dole's central attributes Smith said, "Integrity."

At the time of Dole's death, Smith recalled one of Dole's quotes: "A first-class democracy cannot tolerate second-class citizens." The Dole Institute specifically exists to produce first-class citizens – and in that sense there could be no more fitting memorial to the man from Russell.

(Lawrence, KS, was founded in 1854 by the New England Emigrant Aid Society for the expressed purpose of making Kansas a Free State.)

Sixty years ago — against all odds — Ed Brooke won a historic victory

Sen. Edward Brooke holding the podium gavel during the 1968 Republican National Convention in Miami (Library of Congress)

With the mid-term elections rapidly approaching, I want to take you back 60 years to one of the most remarkable political stories in American history.

And it happened right here in the Bay State.

For it was on November 7, 1962, that Edward W. Brooke became the first African American to be elected to the position of attorney general. Not just the first in Massachusetts history, but the first in any state, ever.

The story of how this came to be is one worth telling.

Brooke, a native of Washington, D.C., first became acquainted with Massachusetts when sent to Ft. Devens for basic training as a consequence of enlisting in the U.S. Army during WWII.

Following distinguished military service, including working behind the lines with Italian partisans, Capt. Brooke decided to return to Massachusetts, where he obtained a law degree from Boston University.

In 1960, he sought and won the Republican nomination for the office of secretary of state. Brooke lost in the general election to a Democrat, Kevin White, an individual who lacked a sense of subtlety by distributing "Vote White" bumper stickers. However, the race was so close — Brooke managed to draw 1.1 million votes despite spending only $17,000 on his entire campaign — that he was identified by the media as someone to keep an eye on.

One person who kept an eye on him was the newly-elected Republican governor, John Volpe. Elected to fight wide-spread corruption at the state level during the Foster Furcolo era, Volpe named Brooke as chair of the Boston Finance Committee to do the same for the equally corrupt city government. Which he did.

As the 1962 election approached, Brooke was invited by Elliott Richardson — a Harvard Law School-trained Boston Brahmin and himself a rising GOP star — to lunch at the Parker House. Richardson's purpose was to tell Brooke that it had been decided by the party establishment that he should run for lieutenant governor.

Brooke told Richardson he wasn't interested. "I intend to be a candidate for attorney general," he said.

Richardson was taken aback. "But, Ed," he said, "I am going to be our candidate for attorney general." Brooke, stung by the condescending, patronizing tone, decided in that very moment it was game on.

Key to winning the nomination was an endorsement by delegates at the GOP pre-primary convention, held in Worcester on Saturday,

June 16. I recall this event vividly, as I was driving with my dad to and from his childhood home in Athol that day and we had the radio tuned to live coverage.

Although just 13, I had developed a real interest in Brooke, much as my parents had. The nominating convention turned out to be an epic nail-biter. At one point, after the first ballot, Richardson was declared the winner by a single vote. It seemed over.

But then a delegate, Francis Wood, notified the chair, U.S. Senator Leverett Saltonstall, that his vote had been misappropriated and that he was voting for Brooke, not Richardson. This meant Richardson failed to reach the threshold needed — again, by one vote. Bedlam ensued. The radio reporter described how Brooke and Richardson forces went out in the darkening streets to drag delegates — who thought things were over — away from bars and restaurants.

It all made great radio drama … with a happy ending, from my perspective.

The Brooke team, led by the legendary Roger Woodworth, proved more adept at reeling in delegates. He won with a comfortable margin. With that official endorsement, went on to beat Richardson in the September primary and then defeated Democrat Francis X. Kelly (best known for his tireless support for a state lottery) in the general election.

Kelly was equally adept at slinging racial mud. At one point, he said on live radio, "Jerry (Williams), you know if I were not a gentleman, I would say that my opponent is a Negro man with a white wife." Brooke, who came on the show directly after, simply said, "Jerry, I married the woman I loved. Kelly's statement is just sad."

Ed Brooke went on to not only become a highly successful attorney general, but, in 1966 — after being told once again by party bigwigs to "wait your turn" — he became the first African American elected by popular vote to the United States Senate, where he became an important voice on issues relating to housing, civil rights, and women's rights. And I was privileged to serve as his press secretary 16 years after listening to that Worcester radio broadcast.

(Bob says that once you've finished reading* Ipswich On My Mind, *you would do well to pick up the late Ed Brooke's autobiography,* Bridging the Divide.*)

How a call from the blimp pimp helped get my career off the ground

Goodyear publicity photo

I was very pleased to see that the *Ipswich Local News* recently reached its semi-annual fundraising goal.

I was even more pleased to read editor John Muldoon's pledge to use a portion of the proceeds to hire summer interns.

Like many of you, I want to keep this wonderful paper a going concern. In addition to writing this column, I donate all of the revenue from the sale of *Ipswich On My Mind* to the paper. My retail outlets — Betsy Frost Designs, Zenobia, and the Ipswich Inn— do the same.

If the monies go to support interns, so much the better.

That's because I got my start as an intern myself. Mind you, I wasn't called an intern back in 1970. Bill Wasserman dubbed me his "summer reporter" and rotated me through his six newspapers as regulars went on vacation. I was paid $90 a week and given $15 in "travel money."

It wasn't much more than I had been making the summer before at Crane Beach. But the experience I gained was invaluable.

I was first sent to the *Danvers Herald*, which was then edited by an Ipswich resident, Bill Castle. While I had some experience on school papers, I was a neophyte when it came to professional journalism. Bill started me with birth notices, weddings, and obituaries.

Among other things, he taught me that all brides are beautiful and that a groom takes care of horses (whereas a bridegroom is a member of a wedding party).

Bill was endlessly patient. Slowly, he transitioned me into actual reporting, including covering town board meetings and social events.

I was one of two full-time reporters. The other, Andrea Couture, was far more qualified. She was adept at reminding me of this. Indeed, she later went on to a senior role at WGBH. But at this moment, she was content to see me as the low person on the totem pole.

One day, a call came for Bill from a PR person working for Goodyear. He said the Goodyear blimp was going to be at Beverly Airport and would the *Herald* like to send a reporter to take a ride?

Bill, I am sure, looked across the office and thought about who would be most expendable. Which is how I got assigned to blimp duty.

As we lifted off from Beverly Airport's tarmac, the PR guy cheerfully asked me where I'd like to go. Ignoring the fact that I was writing for a Danvers paper, I immediately said "Ipswich" and added "over my house, and then down towards Crane's Beach."

At this point, the pilot piped up. "I can take you to the center of Ipswich. I can take you to your house. But I won't be taking you all the way to the beach. There's a pretty strong westerly wind, and our engines aren't all that strong. If the wind tops 30 mph, we'll end up in Ireland."

By which, I think, he meant we'd end up deceased.

So we did go to Ipswich. I could spy Five Corners, Choate Bridge, and my own home tucked up by the Old South Burial Ground. We even made it partway down Argilla Road before heading back. I took notes and photos, the latter using the paper's Nikon camera.

The whole time, the PR guy chirped away about Goodyear and the wonders of the company and its fleet of blimps.

When I got back to the office, I turned in my film and wrote up my story. It was positive. But in it, I did refer to the Goodyear PR guy as the "blimp pimp." Somehow this got by Bill and made it into print.

The day after the paper was published, I got a call … from the PR guy. I was apprehensive, expecting the worst. But, no, he was ecstatic about the coverage. And so, apparently, was Goodyear.

All of which is to say to this year's crop of interns: have fun with it. You may never have a better job in your life — I never did. And if asked to go up in a blimp, check the wind speed first.

(Bob spent four summers as a substitute reporter and editor. He never again got to ride in a blimp.)

Who wants to be Ipswich's official Town Grouch?

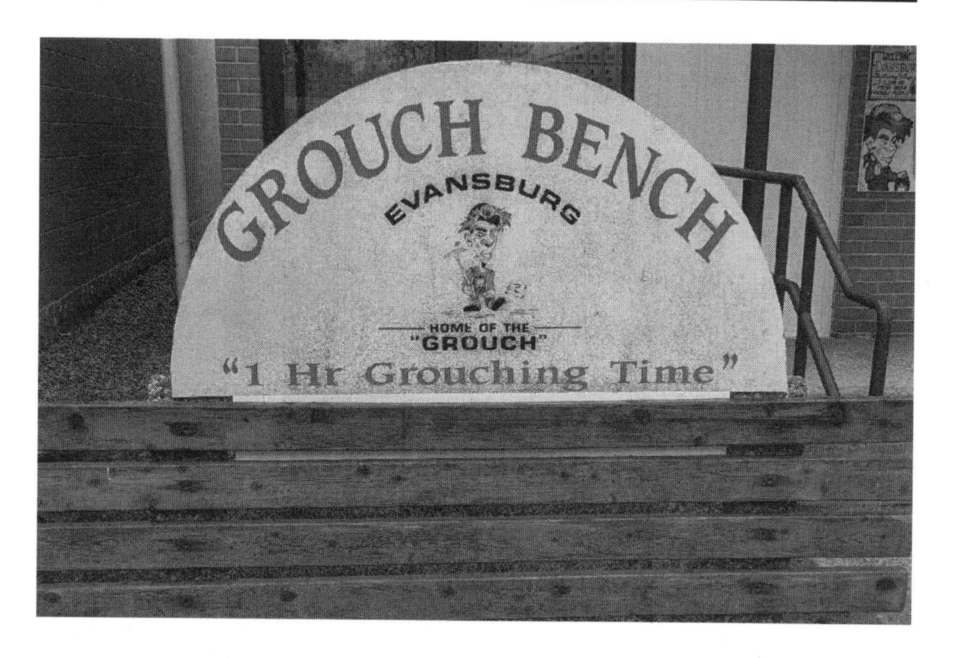

Judging from the tone of recent letters to the editor, not to mention conversations heard on our streets or in various coffee shops and watering holes around town, the good people of Ipswich are in a very grouchy mood.

And it's not just because it is greenhead season. Pretty much everyone is mad about something.

Many would see this as alarming. I, on the other hand, see only opportunity.

Off in faraway Alberta, in a small village called Evansburg, the populace has embraced grouchiness since 1979, naming an official Town Grouch each year.

This tradition apparently started when the person designing a town welcome sign for its outskirts listed its population (603), dogs (29), cats (40) - and still had more room on the sign to fill. In a moment of inspiration, the painter added "Plus one grouch".

Unlike Oscar the Grouch on *Sesame Street*, you didn't have to be a Muppet or live in a trash can. But you did have to be elected and then be available to sit on a dedicated town bench for an hour a day and be grouchy to whomever passed you by. The only limitation imposed by the village was that you could not swear.

It is also significant that the village selected the term grouch over grump. Grump and grumpiness are associated with men of a certain age – think Walter Matthau and Jack Lemmon in the film *Grumpy Old Men* – whereas a grouch can be a man, woman, or anything in between.

Indeed, some of Evansburg's most notable Grouches have been women (but don't ever refer to them as scolds or nags, or they might forget that rule about no swearing).

As far as I can tell, no American town has seized on this brilliant idea. And what better town to do so than Ipswich? Judging by the current town temperament, I would wager that hundreds, if not thousands, of residents would vie for the title. Who wants to be a member of the Select Board when you can boast you're Ipswich's official Town Grouch?

Ipswich already has an official Town Historian; a Town Moderator; a Town Shellfish Constable; and an Animal Control Officer. Why not control the town's prevalent grouchiness by funneling all that negativity into one designated person? This would free up the rest of us to be less like Oscar the Grouch and more like Kermit the Frog.

And much as tiny Evansburg has attained international notoriety for having a Town Grouch, so too might Ipswich. I could see visitors flocking to our town for the sole purpose of being harangued. Indeed, I can see the makings of an annual Grouch Festival, where outsiders vie to out-grouch our official Grouch – a kind of Grouch-off.

There are of course details to be worked out. For example, where to install the grouching bench? Some might favor 5-Corners; others Pine Swamp Road. There's also the County Street Bridge, although conversation would be one-way. My own personal favorite would be outside the Ipswich Local News office on North Main Street.

And how far do we wish to take this? Should we, like the good people of Evansburg, put "Home of the Grouch" on our welcome signs, replacing "Birthplace of American Independence"?

I somehow think Gordon Harris – and the entire Ipswich Historical Commission – might have some reservations about this.

Finally, who should be the inaugural holder of this esteemed title? With Phil Goghen's departure to parts unknown (perhaps Evansburg?), the choice is less obvious than it might have been.

But in case you are wondering, I do not plan to be a candidate. According to my long-suffering spouse, I am a grump, not a grouch.

(Bob recalls that Ipswich once had an official Town Crier. It was discontinued due to the soaring price of Kleenex.)

ChatGPT is going to take my job – and maybe yours

I'm a columnist, and I am pretty sure something called ChatGPT is going to take my job.

And it is going to make one of my other jobs — college professor — infinitely more difficult before it probably takes that one as well.

What is ChatGPT?

ChatGPT — or Chat Generative Pre-Trained Transformer — is a chatbot that was launched by OpenAI, an artificial intelligence research and deployment company, in November 2022.

It is a language model that can generate realistic, human-like text. Like this column.

Indeed, if you asked ChatGPT to write a column in the style of Bob Waite, it will almost instantly do so. And for all you know, that's what it did.

You can ask it to write a sonnet in the manner of Shakespeare extolling the virtues of the Ipswich women's volleyball team, and it will do so. And do it well. Same with a poem in the style of Anne Bradstreet, or a novel in the style of John Updike (with or without the naughty bits).

(Editor's note: We asked for a sonnet, and the results are below).

In Updike's case, perhaps a play? In 1974, he penned *Buchanan Dying*, which revolves around our nation's 15th president, considered by many to be its worst. Why not ask the chatbot to conjure up *Trump Dying* in Updike's style and sell it as a boxed set?

If ChatGPT was just good at mimicking writer's styles, that would be one thing. But it is also extraordinarily adept at conjuring up essays or papers on virtually any topic … and producing an almost infinite number of distinct versions.

Think about that. Let's say an IHS history teacher (or one at Harvard, for that matter) assigned a topic to his or her 30 students. I'll use one everyone jokes about but never actually assigns: "What if Hitler had the bomb? Discuss."

They would receive back 30 different papers, all correctly formatted and footnoted. (Unless, of course, everyone asked for it in the style of Philip K. Dick. In that case they'd get back *The Man in the High Castle*.)

At the college where I teach, I am meant to be preparing students for jobs in public relations, government relations, and investor relations. This is at the graduate level; they all have their first degrees. The ability to write is central to their success. Or, at least, so I thought.

My own son, who is a senior manager at a Minneapolis PR firm, suggests I need to at least rethink that assumption. We may be nearing a time when chatbots like ChatGPT do all of the writing, including press releases, speeches, client pitches, and the like.

PR practitioners (presumably far fewer in number) would be left to more creative tasks, like dreaming up stunts like Rob Gronkowski's Super Bowl "Kick of Destiny."

And what of newspaper columnists? The *New York Times* could probably save some dough pensioning off David Brooks and have the bot write in his style. Same with Howie Carr at the *Herald*.

I will miss teaching and column writing. On the other hand, it'll free up a lot of extra time to hang around the house, something everyone's spouse looks forward to. And I already have a title for my next book, written for me by ChatGPT: *Ipswich Out of My Mind.*

(Bob says the only columnist safe is Doug Brendel, who defies duplication.)

ChatGPT Sonnet – Ipswich Women's Volleyball Team

Oh, Ipswich, Mass., High School Girls' Volleyball team,
Thou art a sight to behold on the court.
With grace and power in each motion beam,
Thou dost leave thy opponents feeling short.

Thy spikes doth soar with beauty and with might,
And every set doth seem a work of art.
Thy serves doth rain like arrows in the night,
And every rally doth pierce the heart.

The teamwork that thou showeth is a sight:
A bond unbreakable, a sisterhood so strong.
With thee, success doth come with such delight,
And every win doth make the praises long.

So here's a sonnet to thee, Ipswich's pride,
A team that truly is both fair and bright!

The 747 — 'Queen of the Skies' — recalls a bygone era never to return

A 1970s view of the lounge in a 747.

Boeing recently announced it had assembled its final 747 jumbo jet and would be delivering it to Atlas Air, a freight carrier, in February. Hearing this brought mixed emotions. It was a great aircraft. But it also possessed a jumbo carbon footprint.

For those of us who have a passion for aviation history, the cessation of the 747 marks the end of an era.

My interest traces back to a patient of my dad's, Pete Williamson. Pete lived in Ipswich and worked as a pilot for Northeast Airlines, based out of Logan Airport.

When I was a kid, I was taken down to Logan and sat in the cockpit of a DC-3 with Pete, who did his best to explain the array of switches and lights.

I was hooked.

Years later, in 1970, Pan Am, the lead customer for the brand-new 747, announced that they were visiting Logan with the launch aircraft. It was a PR stunt — and it worked. I drove to Logan and was not disappointed. The aircraft, with its signature "hump," dwarfed the terminal.

The plane was so big that there was a spiral staircase to reach the upper deck, which in those early days was fitted out by Pan Am with a bar … and a piano! One could imagine Sinatra singing "Fly me to the Moon" with Oscar Peterson tickling the ivories.

My first opportunity to climb on board a 747 came in 1976. I was covering the primaries for a news agency, one with limited funds. I needed to get from the East Coast to my base in San Francisco and learned that Pan Am had a red-eye between the two cities for practically nothing,

At this point, there was no longer a piano bar, and, at any rate, my ticket did not allow me to go up the magic staircase. But the plane was so empty — it was a so-called "dead-head" flight — that I was able to stretch out over four seats and sleep the entire way.

Over the next decade, I had a few more opportunities to climb aboard the 747, as well as rival jumbos like the (to my mind, inferior) L-1011 and the DC-10. But always in coach.

Pan Am 747

Fast-forward to 1981: Out of the blue, I was hired by Big Blue — IBM. My job was to be speechwriter for the CEO of IBM World Trade and other senior executives. Among other things, it meant traveling with them.

In those days, Pan Am was IBM's international carrier. IBM's executives always flew in first or business class.

This was not always exactly relaxing. Sitting next to a company executive for eight or nine hours called for uncharacteristically good behavior.

As it happened, one of my first flights as a newly-minted speechwriter was with the company president, Terry Lautenbach. We were heading from LA to Sydney, which was the site of an IBM board meeting. We were seated in first class, towards the very front of the plane. I was on the window; Terry was on the aisle.

On getting seated, champagne was served in fluted glasses.

We took off. Almost immediately, strange noises emanated from the plane's undercarriage. The pilot started circling over what looked like Catalina Island. He then came on the speaker system. "Ladies and gentlemen, we are unable to confirm that the landing gear has retracted or locked in place. We are dumping our fuel and will shortly be returning to LAX. Please remain calm."

Of course, whenever anyone says, "please remain calm," your blood pressure goes sky-high.

The pilot dumped the fuel. We headed back to LAX. We were told to assume the crash position as the runway — and countless emergency vehicles — rushed into view.

As I bent over, a sticker on my left caught my eye. It was round, silver, and contained Pan Am's marketing slogan of the day in crisp white — "Pan Am: Welcome to a whole new world!"

I nudged Terry and pointed. He laughed.

The landing gear held. We landed safely.

It was at that moment that I realized that whether you were in first class or economy, once you are up at 40,000 feet, everybody is equal in the end.

(Bob says that the 747 was discontinued due to poor fuel efficiency ... and that air travel itself may disappear unless it becomes much more environment-friendly.)

Trapped on a train with thoughts of those left behind

Train at the National New York Central Railroad Museum, Elkhart, Indiana.

The recent "bomb cyclone" that created particular havoc in Buffalo, NY, brought back memories of my grandfather, Joseph Waite.

It was 1969. I was home from college — the University of Wisconsin in Madison — for the holidays. Grampa Waite, who had been living at our South Green home for several years, was not home for the holidays. He lay at Cable Memorial Hospital, dying.

Grandpa was 83. A lifelong smoker, he suffered from emphysema. For those contemplating taking up the habit, consider me your Ghost of Christmas Past and be warned to find a better vice.

As my dad had Cable staff privileges, he could visit grandpa whenever he wished. I would often accompany him. Grandpa was mostly asleep during these visits, and even when he was awake, he said little.

Every day, my dad would carefully shave him and trim his nails — a tick of fastidiousness that reflected his own preferences.

This went on well past Christmas and beyond New Year's. Finally, my dad suggested I'd better head back to school. And given that it was January and the weather forecast ominous, he suggested I take the train.

This meant traveling to Boston's South Station and catching a N.Y. Central train from Boston to Chicago. From there, I could continue on to Madison. Reluctantly, I agreed to abandon the vigil.

In those days, private-sector rail passenger service was on its last legs — and it showed. The rail carriages were antiquated. Freight ruled, with passenger trains frequently shunted aside.

I had a second-class ticket, a generous designation given the shabby condition of the carriage's upholstery and its flickering lights.

Still, traveling by rail did have the feel of adventure. We rumbled through Worcester and Springfield. We stopped in Albany to pick up passengers arriving from N.Y.C.

These newcomers brought new energy, but also tidings of impending doom — a "killer" blizzard was on the way.

Remember that these were different times. No internet. No cell phones. Once on the train, you were isolated from the outside world.

Sure enough, as we progressed through Syracuse and Rochester, what began as a light snowfall evolved into a howling blizzard, one whose gusts rocked our rail car.

The train at first slowed … and then stopped altogether in a place best described as the definition of the middle of nowhere.

And there it sat — not just for hours, but for more than a day. The train's crew, the Southwest Airlines workers of their time, provided no updates or estimates. Nor did they provide food — supplies were exhausted and were to have been replenished in Buffalo.

With the second-class car growing increasingly chilly, I decided to find a better place to starve to death. Making a move worthy of *Titanic*'s Jack Dawson, I bluffed my way into the train's club car — a cozy, wood-paneled rolling tavern.

No one challenged my presence … or my request for a drink and some snacks. What my newfound companions really wanted was a new set of ears to listen to their tales of woe.

One nattily dressed man told me he was on the train due to a fear of flying — and as a result, he was likely to arrive in Chicago too late to be at his mother's bedside before her death.

Postcard of club car in the 1960s

And so it went. A litany of catastrophes worthy of Katherine Anne Porter's novel *Ship of Fools* spilled out from the club car patrons, fueled by gin fizzes or whisky sours.

The scene could have provided a sequel to Porter's best-seller (*Train of Tragedies*).

Eventually, things came back to life. We made it to Buffalo. We pulled into Chicago two days late. As we arrived at Union Station, I jumped off and dashed to a phone booth.

"Operator, I would like to make a collect call to Elmwood 6 – 3433."

My mother accepted the charges. She told me Grandpa had passed away at Cable on January 6.

The truth is, I never really did get to know my grandpa very well. But by staying as long as I did, I got to know my dad better, including observing his simple, almost reverent act of shaving his father's beard. That alone was worth the delay.

(Bob still rides the rails but laments the widespread disappearance of the club car.)

For a fading cohort, JFK's death is still seared into memory

President John F. Kennedy motorcade, Dallas, Texas, Friday, November 22, 1963. Also in the limousine are Jackie Kennedy, Texas Governor John Connally and his wife, Nellie. Library of Congress.

It has been 60 years since John F. Kennedy was shot and killed in Dallas. For those of us alive and old enough to remember, November 22, 1963, remains seared into our memories, much as 9/11 is for younger Americans.

We are a fading cohort. Today, only about one in five Americans have any recollection of where they were at the time of the Kennedy assassination.

But I remember distinctly. I was 14 and in class at the "new" (since demolished) high school. The school had an intercom system, and the news that Kennedy had been shot was relayed from the school office. Hearing this produced a collective gasp — save for one student, who let out a laugh (undoubtedly involuntarily, but it elicited stern sideways glances and a couple of sharp comments).

We were dismissed early. I walked from Linebrook Road through downtown and on to my home on the South Green in a state of dazed disbelief.

Although Ipswich in those days leaned Republican, many of us had identified with Kennedy. He was young (following Dwight Eisenhower, who was decidedly old). He had an attractive family. He was from Massachusetts. Most importantly, in his speeches, he had reached out to a "new generation," which we took to be us.

When I got home, my mother was already glued to the TV, specifically to CBS and Walter Cronkite. Events unfolded in rapid succession — confirmation of the president's death, the swearing in of Vice President Lyndon Johnson as president, the flight of an aircraft ferrying the new president and the body of his slain predecessor to Washington, the apprehension of a suspect — a man named Lee Harvey Oswald.

It seemed all we did that weekend was watch television. Which is how I got to see that same suspect get gunned down on live television on Sunday morning. The Dallas police were transferring Oswald between facilities and somehow let a sketchy character named Jack Ruby get close enough to put a bullet, which proved fatal, into his midsection.

On Monday, we — and virtually everyone else in the nation — watched the funeral, with Jackie and her two children, Caroline, and John-John, bravely trying to hold things together.

The evening before, clergymen from Ipswich's eight churches gathered together with town officials and more than 800 residents in the new high school gym for a short but emotional civic memorial service. At the end, the crowd sang all four verses of "America."

Although we did not fully realize it at the time, the Kennedy assassination turned out to be a pivotal moment for my generation. Coming out of the 1950s, most Americans trusted their institutions, including their government. Foreign policy was conducted on a bipartisan basis. Vietnam had not yet morphed into an American war. Confidence in the media was strong.

But the murky circumstances surrounding Kennedy's death created unease, despite official investigations and explanations. Conspiracy theories abounded. This was a time when my generation lost its innocence and began to increasingly question authority. It is too strong to say that the assassination unhinged young Americans, but it definitely made us see the world as a more dangerous and less predictable place.

All this fed into the unrest of the 1960s, as society ricocheted from racial unrest to war resistance to a rapid-fire spate of assassinations that included Malcolm X, Martin Luther King, and Robert Kennedy. Things had reached such a point that by 1968, the assassination of Robert Kennedy almost felt expected.

So, yes, I am in that dwindling minority that can recall where I was on November 22, 1963. And I believe that event helped shape where we are as a nation in 2023.

(Bob says he never met JFK but did catch a glimpse of him riding in a convertible while he was in Palm Beach in December of 1960.)

Want a stress-free Thanksgiving? Head to a restaurant!

Left is Norman Rockwell's painting Freedom From Want. At right is a modern parody.

"Over the river and through the woods, to grandmother's house we go." – Lydia Maria Child, 1844

This song always reminds me of Thanksgiving. And my dad's mom, whom we called Nana.

She and my grandfather lived in the central part of the state. Sadly, unlike the song's lyrics, we did not travel to see them by sleigh — where the horse knew the way — but by car along Route 2, about two hours west from Ipswich.

And here is where I must make a confession, one that flies in the face of every holiday convention (and every Norman Rockwell depiction of Thanksgiving family gatherings that you've ever seen): My Nana, who in every other way was perfectly wonderful, was a terrible cook.

Even at the age of six or seven, this became apparent pretty quickly as we tucked into her Thanksgiving turkey. It was so dry that it could have gotten a role as an extra in the film *Lawrence of Arabia*.

This really was not her fault. My grandparents were of English and Irish extraction. And while both England and Ireland have undergone something of a culinary renaissance over the past 30 years, they were of a generation that believed in things like New England boiled dinners and spinach from a can.

My parents did not say much in front of us kids on the ride back to Ipswich, but a year later, at Thanksgiving, we found ourselves with our grandparents at a place called Tully Brook Inn in Royalston. The food was great, and Nana seemed pleased — perhaps even relieved.

The following year, it was back to the Tully Brook Inn. A year later, we went to the 1640 Hart House. This time, both Nana and our mom looked pleased and relieved.

Our mom was actually quite a good cook, and she orchestrated dozens of fabulous Thanksgiving, Christmas, and Easter dinners for our family over the years. But thinking back, it took days of preparation, and even with some of us pitching in, it must have been exhausting for her.

Of course, this was back in '50s, '60s, '70s, when women were expected to fulfill what was almost a societal duty.

What about today? According to a recent YouGov survey, men have begun to inch into the Thanksgiving kitchen — but while nearly half of the women report they do all or most of the cooking, only 24% of the males surveyed made that same claim.

And what of Thanksgiving dinner clean-up? Again, women are twice as likely to do the dishes and package up the leftovers as compared to their male counterparts. (This one is interesting. In our household, the person who makes a meal is automatically excused from cleaning up.)

And what about celebrating Thanksgiving at a restaurant? The same survey, taken just after Thanksgiving in 2021, indicated only four percent of Americans went to a restaurant for Thanksgiving. Another two percent ordered takeout or delivery.

Contrast this to Mother's Day or Valentine's Day, which are among the busiest for the restaurant trade.

Previously, I argued that Thanksgiving be moved back to its original October date (knowing full well that it wouldn't happen).

Now I am making the case for going out for Thanksgiving dinner. If nothing else, being in a public space might lessen the chances of one of those inevitable family squabbles over religion, politics ... or somebody's latest piercing or tattoo.

Again, I know this is unlikely to happen. And, at any rate, the Tully Brook Inn is long gone. And Kim at the 1640 Hart House told me they will not be open this Thanksgiving, as they've decided to let their hard-working staff be home with their families.

Of course, there's always the McDonald's drive-thru in Rowley. If the horse knows the way.

(Bob says he cooks the meals at home about once a week. His specialty is tacos.)

Your Social Security eligibility age rose, even as life expectancy fell

Back in 1983, the U.S. government decided to slowly raise the social security retirement age to 67 from 65.

Their logic was that Americans were living a lot longer than was the case back in 1935, when the Social Security Act was implemented. Indeed, life expectancy in the United States had been on an almost continuous upward trajectory for decades.

The change has been implemented gradually.

The full retirement age of 65 applied to those born in 1937 or earlier. Those born between 1943 and 1954 needed to wait until they turned 66 to achieve full retirement age (and get a full payout).

The full retirement age further increased in two-month increments each year until the number reached 67.

That has happened. For those who turned age 62 in 2022 — born in 1960 — 67 is now the magic number. The full retirement age will remain age 67 for everyone born in 1960 or later.

As I say, there was a certain logic to moving up the age of eligibility. It is good to recall that when the world's first government-sponsored social security system was set up in Germany in 1889 by Otto von Bismarck, the "Iron Chancellor" set the age at 65, knowing full well that less than 5% of the population lived that long.

When the administration of President Franklin Roosevelt set up the U.S. program, they, too, set the retirement age of 65, their actuaries undoubtedly aware that many Americans would not cross that finish line.

Which brings us back to life expectancy.

Since 2015, according to the U.S. Center for Disease Control and Prevention (CDC), the United States has seen a historic decline in life expectancy, in part driven by the opioid epidemic and, beginning in 2020, the COVID-19 pandemic. Other factors across the time period included an increase in accidents, homicides, and individuals taking their own lives.

Not unexpectedly, the last two years marked the biggest drop in a century, going back to the influenza pandemic of 1918, with expectancy sinking to 76.1 years, down from an average of 79 years in 2019. COVID was directly responsible for at least half of this decline, according to Claire Klobucista, writing recently in *Foreign Affairs* magazine.

Which, of course, leaves us with the other half of the decline: things such as opioid deaths and murders. Will a lessening of COVID bring a return to increased U.S. life expectancy? Time will tell.

But one thing we can be sure of is that social security age requirements will not be rolled back to match the decline. Things just don't work that way, even though increasing longevity was the central argument for the change (along with the stabilizing the financial viability of the system itself).

Speaking of financial viability, I just received a notice from the Social Security Administration that, beginning this month, my benefit will increase by 8.7% because of a rise in the cost of living.

I am grateful for the increase, but I worry that it is, in effect, being financed by all those Americans who came off the rolls prematurely over the past five years.

(Bob says he actually elected to take Social Security early. To paraphrase Mickey Mantle, had he known he'd live this long, he would have elected to take better care of himself.)

Ipswich is not Wenham; Ipswich is not Boxford; Ipswich is Ipswich

The Ipswich Mills used to be a lot bigger than EBSCO (via HistoricIpswich.org)

Ipswich is not Wenham. Ipswich is not Boxford.

Don't get me wrong. Wenham and Boxford are lovely little towns. And they work hard to keep it that way.

But neither exactly embraces commerce. Yes, Wenham has its teahouse and a ski and tennis shop, but residents need to head to South Hamilton or North Beverly to encounter the hurly-burly of business. Boxford is much the same.

Ipswich, on the other hand, has been a town interested in business and commerce from the moment the earliest Puritan settlers constructed the first dam on the Ipswich river in 1637.

Ipswich settlers made things, be it pillow lace or shoes. It is telling that the Rev. Nathaniel Ward's 1647 satiric work of fiction, "The Simple Cobbler of Agawam," featured a tradesman, rather than a farmer, as its protagonist.

Commerce could also be found at the town wharf, whether it be the hauling in of the then-ample fish stocks of Ipswich Bay or the hauling out of timber and other resources for export.

And so it continued. Industrial plants, including Hayward Hosiery, the Ipswich Mills, and Sylvania hugged the Ipswich River. With them came immigrants — many from Poland, Greece, and French-Canada — looking for work and enriching the town's cultural heritage.

Because Ipswich was a considerable distance from places like Salem and Newburyport (and, of course, Boston), downtown developed as its own trading center, with banks, dry-goods stores, pharmacies, groceries, and the like.

Over the years, Ipswich had its own theater (the Strand), three auto dealerships (Ford, Chevrolet, and Rambler), numerous garages and gas stations, restaurants, and a hotel (the Hayes). Not to mention more drinking establishments per capita than any other city or town in Massachusetts.

In some ways, the crown jewel of downtown, established in 1923, was Hill's Men's Shop (later Hill's Family Store). I say, "crown jewel" not just because the Market Street store anchored downtown, but because its owner, Howard "Taffy" Hill, was an example of the good a business can do.

Although he never talked much about it or sought the spotlight, it became well known that if calamity befell an Ipswich family, Taffy would be there to help. More than once, when a home burned down, he would quietly outfit the entire family with clothing.

"He was just born with that sense of generosity," his son, Brad Hill, said at the time of Taffy's death in 2011.

But Taffy was not unique. Many other business owners contributed to the community, either directly or through involvement in service organizations like Rotary, Kiwanis, or the Lions Club. The roll is a long one — companies like Ipswich Shellfish, Tedford & Martin,

Quint's, Conley's, Elliott Fuel, Marcorelle's, McCormack & Son, Strand Furniture, Tetreault Jewelers, and on and on.

Some are still with us. Others, like Hill's Family Store, are gone. But my point is that embracing business and commerce not only provided employment for residents but did — and still does — much good for our community.

A prime example is EBSCO, which today occupies the Sylvania site and a number of other buildings downtown. The company is the poster child for good corporate citizenship, including the EBSCO Community Impact Fund, which allocates money to local not-for-profits.

There is also now Ora, whose CEO, Stuart Abelson, just made possible the return of Ipswich's long-gone 1934 Seagrave fire truck. Given all the controversy around Ora's request to locate a facility on Waldingfield Road, a cynic might see this as simply a PR stunt. But I think of it differently — as yet another act of generosity by an individual engaged in commerce in our town.

Yes, Ipswich is not Wenham. Ipswich is not Boxford. Ipswich is Ipswich. And that is a good thing.

(Bob still hasn't gotten over the closing of Hill's Family Store, the Strand Theater, and Quint's Drug Store.)

Charles III, a man of passionate opinion, may find the crown a confining burden

Prince Charles, Princess Diana at Treasure Houses (public domain image)

Shakespeare, in *Henry IV*, tells us, "Uneasy is the head that wears a crown." This observation today is often rendered as, "Heavy is the head that wears the crown."

I do not know which version King Charles III prefers — or if he has any preference at all.

But he certainly has had a great deal of time to think about it. At 73, Charles is the oldest person to accede to the throne in British history. Put another way, he was a king-in-waiting for virtually his entire life.

Due to an odd set of circumstances, I have twice spent time with the newly-minted monarch.

The first came on a November Saturday morning in 1985. I was working for Ford Motor Company in their Washington, D.C., office at the time.

Ford of Europe's vice chair, a man named Walter Hayes, had conjured up an exhibit called "Treasure Houses of Britain" for America's National Gallery. It comprised all manner of items, from paintings to furniture to tapestries, drawn from the great estates of the realm's most prominent families.

The exhibit was to be officially opened to the public on Sunday, November 3, by the Prince of Wales and Princess Diana. However, a day prior to that, there was to be a private viewing — just the prince and princess, National Gallery head J. Carter Brown, and someone from Ford.

Thanks to the generosity of my boss, Jerry terHorst, that someone turned out to be me. Jerry is best known for resigning as Gerald Ford's press secretary at the time of the Nixon pardon. But, to me, for this and numerous other reasons, it is his kindness that I recall.

As you might expect, I had to be vetted by palace authorities prior to gaining access to the royals. Hence, a visit to my office by a security person. His first words were, "Mr. Waite, we know who you are!" This was off-putting because, at the age of 36, I still was not sure myself.

He went on to tell me that an ancestor, Thomas Waite, had, in 1649, signed the death warrant for King Charles I. Fortunately, the investigator was just playing with me. "I think we can put that in the past," he offered with a smile.

Thus cleared, I spent about two hours with Charles and Diana wandering around the West Wing of the Gallery. Carter Brown — clearly the master of the building and his subject matter — did most of the talking. I answered a couple of questions regarding Ford's sponsorship role and engaged in some pleasantries.

My impression was of a couple who were happy to be with each other. I could not help but notice Diana's youth, a certain kind of beauty, and her apparent need to appear to be no taller than her husband (as expressed by her choice of shoes). It was Charles who asked most of the questions. They both appeared quite interested in what they were seeing and were reserved, but not stuffy.

My second encounter with Charles came in 2009. I was by now an executive at Canada Post, in charge of the crown corporation's Social Responsibility (ESG) activities. Charles was visiting Canada and had asked to meet with a small number of representatives of business, government, and environment advocacy organizations in a roundtable discussion.

Attendees included, among others, a very young Justin Trudeau … and me.

Of course, much had changed since 1985. Charles and Diana's marriage had gone off the rails, and Diana had met her tragic end in a Paris tunnel. Charles, by now, had turned his attention elsewhere — including to issues of the day.

During the two-hour session, Charles was articulate, knowledgeable, and spoke with real passion. It was apparent he cared genuinely about the environment, including topics like sustainable agriculture and species and habitat protection. He exhibited a head full of opinions and ideas. He was, in short, impressive.

Now he is king. It is a job that requires great restraint and little opportunity for personal expression. Given the passion I saw that day, the crown, for Charles, may prove to be very heavy indeed.

(Bob does not know too much about his ancestor, Thomas "the Regicide" Waite, but he suspects this may have accounted for a dearth of Buckingham Palace invites over the years.)

Who wants to be a millionaire? In Massachusetts, maybe no one

When I was a student at the University of Wisconsin, during the days of radical protest in the late '60s, I would occasionally see the slogan "Eat the rich" scrawled in bright red paint on campus walls.

My first thought was that someone was cleverly playing off Jonathan Swift's satiric essay "A Modest Proposal" — but with fat-cat millionaires substituting for Irish children.

My second thought was that the revolution was not being led by vegetarians.

All of this came to mind the other day when I was filling out my Massachusetts election ballot and came to Question 1.

Put succinctly, Question 1 proposes amending the state's constitution by mandating an additional 4% tax (on top of the current 5%) on any income above $1 million.

Massachusetts, it would seem, doesn't want to eat the rich — it just wants to nibble them to death.

At this juncture, I do have to make a confession: I was once a millionaire.

This was back in 1977. By local standards I was fabulously wealthy.

I was living in Warsaw at the time and had translated my meagre funds — $10,000 U.S. — into Polish zlotys. I did so via the black market, where a dollar was worth 100 zloty, not the five zloty posted by the then-communist government.

Presto — I was a zloty millionaire!

It was not a terribly risky transaction. Even high-ranking government officials availed themselves of the black market.

But in terms of real money — dollars — I never breached the $1 million barrier. And unless they start paying professors seven-figure salaries (or some future book of mine becomes a best-seller and I option the movie rights to Brad Pitt), I never will.

So this Question 1 amendment has no impact on me. But it definitely does leave me puzzled.

First of all, why amend the constitution? And if you must do so, why be so specific? At the rate things are going in terms of galloping inflation, in another decade or so, earning $1 million might not be all that unusual.

Second, if you're going to soak the rich, why be so half-hearted? Where does the number 4% come from? This looks less like a soaking and more like a light drizzle, just enough to annoy people.

According to a Tufts University study, only about 26,200 Massachusetts households will break the $1 million threshold in 2023. And about half will do so primarily because they've sold a business they've created or a farm, investment property, or restaurant.

So, part of me says, "Hey, what the heck — it's only 26,200 households. If they don't like it, they can move to New Hampshire or Florida." Except that another part of me remembers that I actually know dozens of Massachusetts residents who have already moved to places like Portsmouth or Sarasota … and that maybe losing more these folks is not a great idea.

People with a bit of wealth are the people who disproportionately support things like PBS, hospitals, educational institutions, and various arts programs. If they flit off to Florida or New Hampshire, they'll still probably have an interest in the theater, symphony, or PBS programming — but they might simply now channel that interest into their new local community.

As I say, this question will not affect me personally. I actually pay far higher tax rates than anything we are talking about here. My Canadian federal tax rate is 26.5%; my Ontario rate is 11.16%; on top of that, I am taxed 13% — a VAT — on virtually everything I purchase; and on top of that, I pay the U.S. Alternative Minimum Tax (just in case there is anything left over).

In short, I'm a tax-paying fool.

But when it comes to Question 1, I do wonder if eating the rich makes any more sense in 2022 than it did in 1968. I see indigestion ahead.

(Bob doesn't mind paying high taxes, snug in the knowledge that someday Canada might actually have a national defense force.)

How working as a paper boy (almost) made a man of me

When I was seven or eight, I was given a set of block letters, the kind you could use to print using an ink pad. These came to me from my mom's side via a great uncle, Joseph Heade, who worked for the *St. Louis Post-Dispatch*.

With this newfound treasure, I promptly composed and printed a newspaper, selling copies to my younger siblings for two cents.

The enterprise failed after two editions. I am not sure which ran out first — my brother's and sister's pennies or my own patience in hand-composing the individual issues.

All of this comes to mind as the U.S. and Canada celebrate "National Newspaper Week" October 2 through 8. Now in its 82nd year, it is meant to get us to reflect on the vital role newspapers and their employees play in fostering a functioning democracy.

Of course, much has changed since 1940, when Newspaper Week debuted. The number of papers has plummeted. Readership peaked in 1984, and decline accelerated with the advent of the internet and streaming services. Today, when I ask students their primary news source, most name Reddit.

One way to understand just how much things have changed involves taking you back to my days as a paper boy.

When I was about 12 or so, I had a paper route. Early each morning, at about 6:30 a.m., I would trundle down to the long-gone Ipswich News Store on Market Street. The News Store was what one would term "atmospheric." The air was heavy with the aroma of pipe tobacco and reverberated with the sounds of its owners barking out commands.

Once you got past the tobacco and the vintage postcards, you found yourself in a spare back room with a long counter. There, you were meant to carefully count out your allotment. I had 54 papers to deliver. The trick was to get things exactly right, as a wrong count meant returning to the store for a stern lecture ... and a deduction from your week's meager wages.

My route ran from just over Choate Bridge to Southern Heights. It included my own South Green home. The papers were arranged in a canvass bag nestled in an oversized basket attached to the front of my bicycle. This was no Masi Gira Mondo — a Schwinn, it had just one gear and a coaster-brake.

Even today, when I pass by houses on South Main, Elm, Poplar, Ward, Argilla, Payne, County, Southern Heights, or South Village Green, I can still recall which house got which paper. And there was quite a variety of papers, which complicated matters.

They included the *Boston Globe*, *Herald*, and *Record*; the *Lawrence Eagle-Tribune*; the *New York Times*; and the *Christian Science*

Monitor. A few customers even received two newspapers, perhaps reflecting differing political sensibilities among household members.

I even recall who tipped well and those who did not. I was fortunate to have several doctors and a judge on my route, including two who tipped a dollar each week — a fortune in the early 60s. (My dad tipped 50 cents, still a goodly amount when most gave you a quarter, a dime, or nothing at all). In an average week, I netted about $12. To put that in perspective, back then you could get a clam plate for $3.95 (I had my own peculiar way of assessing relative value).

Delivering papers very early in the morning was not without its little surprises, such as the time a middle-aged woman appeared at the door of a house on South Main, near the River Walk bridge, wearing nothing more than a smile — an event that advanced my knowledge of human anatomy far beyond what I had gleaned previously from *National Geographic* and perusing purloined medical texts.

Putting aside the monetary and educational value, delivering papers taught me about the desire my neighbors had to get news from a source they deemed trustworthy.

Today, newspaper boys (and girls) are long gone. To the extent home delivery exists at all, it is typically done by adults driving vintage Datsuns or slightly newer Kias.

All of which is to say that Ipswich is blessed to have a paper delivered to every home by the U.S. Postal Service. During National Newspaper Week, that is certainly something worth celebrating.

(Bob once took on an afternoon route in addition to his morning one to spell his next-door neighbor. This lasted only two weeks, as both he and his Schwinn eventually collapsed.)

Keeping to the straight and narrow on the Canal du Midi

HOMPS, FRANCE — Have you seen those ads for Viking Cruises on the Danube or the Rhine? The ones with passengers lounging in luxury as crew members cater to their every need?

Put that image out of your mind.

We are on the Canal du Midi. Finished in 1681, this UNESCO World Heritage site was (and is) an engineering marvel, linking the Mediterranean Sea with the Atlantic.

Its role in conveying goods ceased by the end of World War II. Today, it carries would-be captains cruising in specially fitted-out craft.

Fully 10,000 boats make their way up and down its 149-mile length each year.

Our boat is 44 feet long and, in theory, sleeps six, although this would require all six to be contortionists or experts at spooning.

We are, however, only three — my spouse (Karen), her sister (Jodi), and me. A cousin, Shaun, has dropped out due to some sort of domestic calamity (or, more likely, a premonition).

Having plied the waters of Ipswich Bay in my youth on my dad's 22-foot craft, including successfully navigating the Essex, Parker, and Ipswich rivers, I reasoned that captaining a boat on a canal would be a breeze. If nothing else, it would be difficult to get lost.

My first clue that I might be mistaken in this assumption came when I examined our boat more closely.

It was festooned all around with heavy, black rubber strips. Hung at intervals along the hull were bulbous, black bumpers.

This had the effect of making the boat look more like one of those bumper-car rides you'd find at an amusement park.

The company renting the craft, Le Boat, had sent out a video in advance, one I actually watched. They also provided a kind of online manual which, identifying as a male, I completely ignored.

We were taken out for a test run by a whippet-thin woman named Mimi, who repeatedly told me that I would do just fine — even as I began to fishtail in the strong breeze.

"Yes, it is windy like this 300 days a year," she cheerfully allowed, "but you'll get used to it."

I did not get used to it. I also discovered that a 44-foot boat handles quite differently than one that clocks in at a mere 22 feet.

And that side-thrusters — jets of water that move you laterally left or right — take a bit of practice.

The reason for all of the bumpers, side-thrusters, and obligatory manual-reading soon became apparent as we headed out.

The canal is straddled by numerous bridges, many dating from the 17th century.

Built of stone and with arches so low that standing up on the bridge would get you KO'd, they are barely wide enough to accommodate one boat at a time.

Think of the spans under Choate Bridge — and subtract a yard or two.

A combination of a wind gust, too much speed, and frantic side-jet toggling caused the boat to bounce side-to-side off the walls of the first bridge. It was like being inside a pinball machine.

We did not go down with the ship, but we did lose one of our bulbous bumpers.

All that was left, in mute testimony, was a swaying, severed, blue nylon rope.

And then there were the locks. Lots and lots of locks. While we did not nearly do them all — there are 74 that drop you 620 feet as you travel eastwards — each must be carefully choreographed, as typically three boats share space in the lock as you are moved upwards or downwards.

Again, as with the bridges, there was a steep learning curve. Fortunately, unlike their captain, my crew of two were quick to figure out how to secure the ropes and where to step when.

All of this seemed to entertain the lock-keepers as well as other boat crews.

After the initial teething issues, things settled down. We moored on the banks of lovely villages some nights, enjoying the local cuisine and visiting a chateau, church, or, in one instance, an enormous canal-side bookstore boasting 50,000 titles.

At other times, we pulled off (to quote Mimi) "in full nature," mooring under southern French skies.

I would recommend the trip. Once you get past your first moments of sheer terror, the experience is relaxing and good for the soul (if not the waistline).

But for those of you who pride yourself on your prowess navigating the sandbar off Crane's or the mouth of the Ipswich or Essex rivers, take it from me — read the captain's manual!

(Bob was shocked to learn that* Ipswich On My Mind *was not stocked among the 50,000 titles at the Canal du Midi bookstore.)

The River Jordan is no longer deep and wide and the Dead Sea is dying

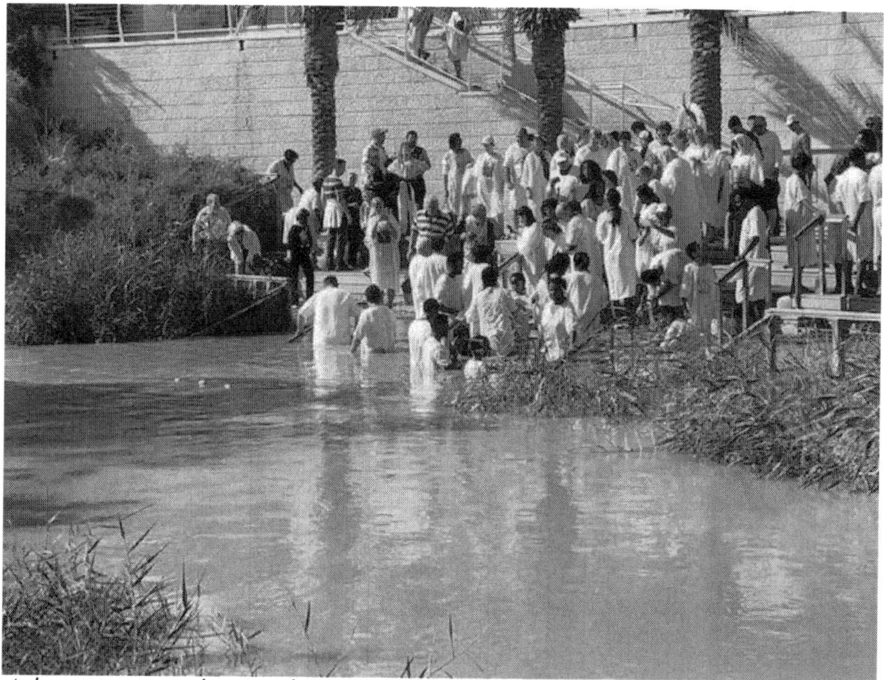

A baptism on the Jordan River (Bob Waite photo)

"The River Jordan is deep and wide. Milk and honey on the other side."

BETHANY BEYOND THE JORDAN — Perhaps, in 1960, when the Highwaymen had a hit with "Michael Rowed the Boat Ashore", the River Jordan was indeed deep and wide.

But it is neither today. I am standing on the East Bank in Jordan. The West Bank — the Israeli side — could be reached by skipping a stone across the water's surface.

Not that I would recommend doing that, as armed military are visible on both shores.

As I gaze on this diminished waterway, I can't help but think of another — the Ipswich River — which has thrice been designated one of America's most endangered. .

I also recall being on the Mekong in Laos in early 2020 and learning from our guide that that river, too, is being strangled by a combination of new dams upriver and reduced runoff at its mountain headwaters.

Much the same can be said of the Ganges. And in the U.S., we have the example of the Colorado, whose waters are redirected to the arid west. Fresh water, too often taken for granted, is becoming an increasingly scarce strategic resource — the new oil.

Some of this is due to climate change. Mountain glaciers are melting away. When they are gone, river flows will drop significantly.

But some of it is due to human activity and politics. The Jordan is a good example. There is a lot of Middle East-style finger-pointing, but, in truth, while Israel over several decades has taken the lion's share from the river proper, Syria and Jordan have also contributed to the problem by diverting much water from important tributaries.

By the time the Jordan reaches the Dead Sea, it is a mere trickle. The result is a body of water that is visibly shrinking. In 1995, I visited the Dead Sea on the Israeli side. It had already dropped so much that boardwalks providing access to that sea had been extended hundreds of yards, leaving facilities, including spas, stranded.

Things have only gotten more dire. Visiting "Panorama Dead Sea," a Japanese-funded education center perched high on the Jordanian side, you can look at a model of the sea that traces its decline chronologically … or you can simply go outside to a viewpoint and see the receding watermarks on the shore, as visible as the rings in a bathtub.

For Jordan, one of the driest nations on earth, the problem is acerbated by population growth. In the period from 1960 to today, the population of that country went from 900,000 to 11 million, an eye-popping 1,000 percent increase. Much of it was fueled by refugees streaming from Palestine and, more recently, Syria.

Other water-challenged countries, like India and Pakistan, have also experienced significant population growth. Just recently, the UN announced the world's population had reached eight billion.

Before this all becomes too depressing, there are some signs of hope on the horizon.

Two weeks ago, Israel and Jordan signed a water-for-energy agreement in Sharm el Sheikh as part of the UN Climate Conference. It involves sending energy derived from solar to Israel in exchange for water produced by Israel's advanced desalination plants.

When news of the agreement came out, it resulted in demonstrations in Jordan's capital, Amman, by those opposed to any kind of cooperation with Israel. But with any luck, the cooperative agreement will go forward.

If Israel and Jordan can find a path to a more sustainable water regime, perhaps something can be done about the excessive groundwater withdrawals affecting the Ipswich River. Surely the 14 communities served by the river — several lying outside its watershed — can come up with a solution that keeps the river flowing? One can hope.

It would be nice to see the Ipswich River once again deep and wide — to which Ipswich River Watershed Association's Wayne Castonguay would undoubtedly respond, "Hallelujah"!

(Bob passed on an opportunity to be re-baptized in the Jordan's waters, but he did buy some Dead Sea mud.)

The Holy Land is a holy mess – but the Nativity story still inspires

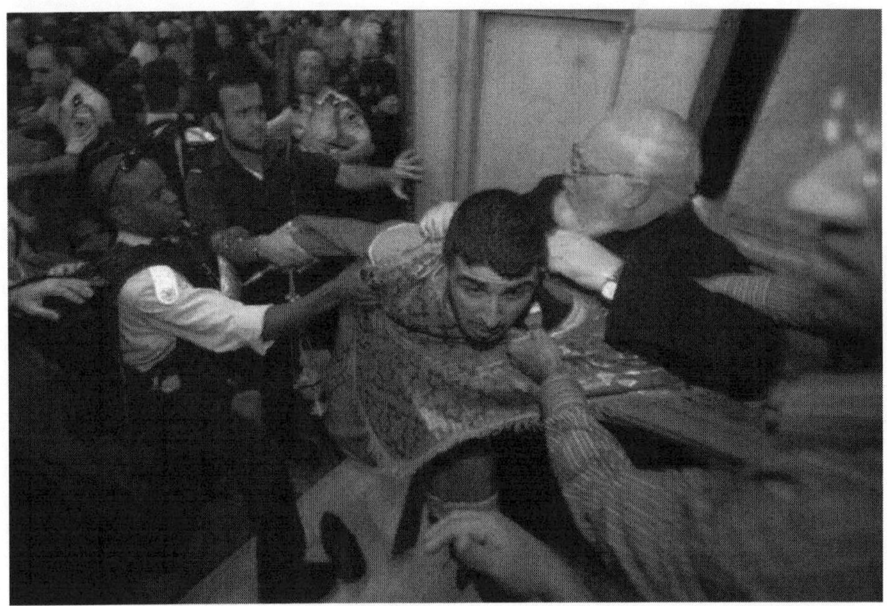

Monks brawling

MOUNT NEBO — If you visit Mount Nebo in Jordan, you can catch the same glimpse of the Promised Land that Moses did. And you can do so without the inconvenience of dying soon after.

Moses is said to be buried somewhere in the vicinity of the 2,230-foot ridge, located high above the Dead Sea.

The Bible says he had been told by God that he could lead his people out of captivity but would not be allowed to cross over to a land of milk and honey.

Christians, Muslims, and Jews — all "People of the Book," a reference their shared Old Testament heritage — visit the site. As do those of a non-religious persuasion (perhaps trying to figure out what all the fuss is about).

The thing about visiting the Holy Land — whether it be in Jordan or Israel — is that there can be a lot of fuss. Not to mention commercialization.

For example, there are two dueling baptism sites on the Jordan River associated with John the Baptist: one in Israel and one in Jordan. The one on the Israeli side, in particular, does a thriving business.

The only problem is that the actual place where John performed baptisms (as certified by UNESCO and by Catholic, Orthodox, and secular scholars) lies on dry land about 300 meters away on the Jordan side.

How can this be? Because, over the course of several millennia, river channels shift and move about.

Speaking of moving about, you may recall the biblical story of Salome, step-daughter of King Herod, who danced so fetchingly that Herod said he'd grant her any wish.

What Salome wished for was the head of John the Baptist on a silver platter. And when it was delivered, having been spurned by him while he was living, she proceeded to kiss his disembodied head passionately on the lips.

You can learn all about this at the Shrine of the Beheading of St. John the Baptist, in nearby Madaba, for a small admission fee.

On the Israeli side, which I visited a number of years ago, confusion and counter-claims abound. In Jerusalem, for example, the Church of the Holy Sepulchre, built above what many believe to be the place where Jesus was entombed following crucifixion, has a rival: the so-called Garden Tomb.

The church itself demonstrates the fractious state of Christendom, with sharp-elbowed Armenian, Latin, and Greek sects all jostling for position and advantage. Just for good measure, there is an Ethiopian sect residing on the roof.

Mount Nebo, Jordan.

Also in Jerusalem is Mary's Tomb, where the mother of Jesus was laid to rest by the 12 apostles, who supposedly reconvened to be present for her earthly departure.

On the other hand, when I was in Turkey in 2018, I was told that St. John took Mary to Ephesus for reasons of safety. I was shown her house.

The implication was that she lived out her last days in that country. You pays your money and you takes your choice.

Then there is Bethlehem and Manger Square. Getting to Bethlehem, which lies within the occupied West Bank, requires running the gauntlet of Israeli security, a necessary precaution.

But once in Manger Square, you run another gauntlet: vendors selling every sort of knick-knack. If you find yourself needing a baby Jesus bobble-head, this is the place.

The Church of the Nativity, built over what is thought to be the site of Jesus' birth, shares the fractious management issues endemic to the Holy Sepulchre.

Things got so bad between Greeks and Armenian Christians that, in 1984, a violent clash broke out, with monks from both sides pulling out clubs and chains from beneath their robes.

If you've read this far, you're probably thinking I'm advising against visiting the Holy Land. Not at all. It is a fascinating, compelling place, one that sums up human aspirations, contradictions, and foibles.

As for Christmas, I am drawn back to the simple story of the Nativity, as expressed in the crèche of my youth on display at the old St. Joseph's Church on Mt. Pleasant Street.

It spoke of humble beginnings and promised great hope. There was no price of admission — and no Jesus bobble-heads to be seen.

(Bob never quite got used to the cavernous Our Lady of Hope Church that superseded St. Joseph's, but he still takes solace in the Nativity story.)

Remembering the real heroes of the three wise men story — the camels!

Bob and Karen cruising around the desert.

WADI RUM — For me, the most intriguing part of the Christmas story involves the three Wise Men, or Magi. And their camels, the "ships of the desert."

The Magi only appear in Matthew's gospel, but they have inspired Christmas carols such as "We Three Kings" … and endless speculation regarding who they really were and where exactly they came from.

Some scholars say Yemen or elsewhere on the Arabian peninsula, based on the gifts — gold, frankincense, and myrrh — that they carried. Others guess Persia.

But what scholars do agree on is that if they crossed expansive deserts to reach Bethlehem, they almost certainly came by camel. And they most likely came through Wadi Rum, or Petra, in what is now Jordan.

Camels are often omitted from Christmas manger scenes and pageants. These are incredibly large animals, so while you might spy the odd child playing the part of a sheep or a shepherd, I have yet to see anyone playing the role of a dromedary (the correct name for single-humped Middle Eastern camels) in a church pageant.

Which is unfortunate. What aspiring thespian wouldn't want to add "camel" to his or her acting resume?

If nothing else, it could be great practice for eventually playing Quasimodo in a revival of *The Hunchback of Notre Dame*. Or Igor in *Young Frankenstein*.

My fascination with camels caused me to climb aboard one at the Pyramids of Giza (with my younger brother, Tom) back in the 1980s. It was a simple photo op, but the handler did tell us to be careful, as camels can bite — or spit in your general direction.

Curious to find out more, a bit of research turned up that these are highly intelligent animals … and that their spitting is usually targeted at persons whom they find annoying.

I also found out they have three sets of eyelids and two sets of eyelashes, that they can completely close their nostrils during sandstorms, and they can drink up to 40 gallons of water to quench their thirst.

As Omar Sharif explained to Peter O'Toole in the film *Lawrence of Arabia*, camels can "go for 21 days in the desert without water. And then they die. And then you die."

While I had no ambition to die in the desert — with or without a camel — I was so intrigued by the species that a few years later, when driving in Israel's Negev desert with my spouse, Karen, we stopped to observe some.

The trouble was that they, in turn, observed us. And one large male, with legs so long they would have made a Radio City Rockette jealous, did more than observe — he made a beeline for me.

He didn't spit. Indeed, his intents were clearly amorous. I knew I was in real trouble when he fetchingly batted his sets of eyelashes. I ran. He ran. I ran faster.

He ran faster still. All the while, I could hear Karen laughing uproariously. Eventually, I found a fence and put it between me and the 1,200-pound beast.

I instantly decided to never again splash on Paco Rabanne cologne prior to encountering a male camel.

I also decided I would henceforth view camels from a distance.

But that changed recently. Karen has a disconcerting habit of springing little surprises on me when we travel. For example, when we visited Victoria Falls in Zimbabwe, she secretly made arrangements for us to zip-line — zig-zagging 12 times! — over the thousand-foot gorge.

This time, the surprise was a 5:30 a.m. camel ride to view the sunrise from a distant Wadi Rum vantage point. As it turned out, it was a wonderful experience.

My camel was well-behaved. No spitting and no romantic advances. Just a pleasant swaying back-and-forth and up-and-down.

I still don't know if the three Wise Men story is factually true, but I do know they were wise to pack gold, frankincense, and myrrh — and leave their Paco Rabanne cologne at home.

(Bob wants people to know that no camels were injured in the writing of this column.)

Late season fishing

The author's mother sensibly driving the "Kant Waite" in warm weather.

With apologies to T.S. Eliot, the cruelest month in Ipswich is not April, but November.

The days grow ever shorter; the beach is depopulated; and, by month end, boating in and around Ipswich Bay is over. At least for most. There were also the die-hards, my dad among them.

Boating – and in particular, fishing – was central to his being. He had selected Ipswich as the place to establish his dental practice based on its seaside location, figuring it was better to fight tooth decay in a location featuring salt air and schooling fish.

Our first boat was a 16 1/2-foot wooden runabout built by Maine's White Canoe Company. He named the boat "Kant Waite" because, well, he couldn't wait.

He trailed that boat, launching it from the Ipswich Outboard Club ramp on Water Street.

Our family's lives, from late spring until well into autumn, were dependent on tide charts. Even for a boat that small, the Ipswich River could be treacherous as the tide went out. Mussel beds threatened props; other stretches were so shallow that you risked getting hung up until the tide turned.

Once free of the river's clutches, he would deposit some family members at Steep Hill or Back Beach and, with one or two of us remaining onboard, head out to seek strippers, blues, or mackerel.

Where we headed was dependent on who he had in his dental chair during a given week. Dad knew who the good fisherman were. He also knew people were more inclined to impart closely held secrets to someone with a whirring drill poised above. If the stripped bass were running on Middle Ground, or near the Spindle, or Bass Rocks, his inquiring mind wanted to know.

Armed with this intelligence, he would head to the designated spot.

Stacey Pedrick, of the band "The Fools", reminisced with me about these practices recently. His dad, Varnum Pedrick, was another stalwart fisherman. Stacey recalled a time when he headed out at the crack of dawn with his dad to rendezvous with mine and with a member of the Marcorelle clan. Three boats converging on a supposed fishing hot spot.

Did anyone catch anything? The answer is lost in the mists of time – and the fog off Plum Island.

Some years later our dad traded in his White for a 22-foot Cruiser, a fiberglass inboard-outboard needing less maintenance, but deeper water. He took to mooring it, first at Perley's Marina in Rowley, later at Pike's in Essex.

Dad's desire to maximize fishing seasons did not abate, often to the annoyance of marina operators, who wanted everybody out by a certain date. They would remind him it was time to wrap things up; he would ignore them.

Early one November day he decided to head out again into the Bay to try his luck. Perhaps he had a hot tip – although by this point, it was only the clammers and a few pulling lobster traps who were still venturing out. At any rate, my brother Tom and I were dragooned into crewing. We ended up near Middle Ground.

We threw an anchor and let the outgoing tidal current create a trolling effect. I don't recall a single strike. But I do recall that as we tried to leave, our anchor line somehow got tangled around our propeller. Really tangled.

The only way out of this dilemma, my dad reasoned, was for someone to go into the water and untangle things. And as my brother Tom was eight years younger (and a foot shorter), the person to do this was me.

I went in. The water came up to my chest. Keep in mind that Ipswich Bay is never warm – but at this time of year, it was truly freezing, Jack Dawson *Titanic* freezing; Ted Williams cryogenic-head freezing.

I somehow freed up the prop. Climbing back onto our boat's deck, the lower half of my body was purple and, more disturbingly, parts of me that were supposed to be outside had retreated inside.

Dad relented. Perhaps seeing his opportunity to become a grandparent slipping away, he declared it was time to pull the boat from the water and call it a season.

(Bob never again ventured out that late but does recall taking a plunge at Crane's in April, which wasn't any better.)

Publishing is like making bratwurst; messy, but relished in the end

It all began innocently enough.

A friend told me that some fellow named John Muldoon had started up a newspaper in my hometown. And that he was being aided and abetted by my first publisher, Bill Wasserman. At the age of 92, Bill had apparently roared out of retirement to be both the paper's consulting guru and itinerant ad salesperson.

I was stunned. Who in their right mind would start a newspaper in the 21st century? Did they not yet know that printed newspapers are dead, consigned to history's scrap heap, along with Kodak film, eight-track tapes, and rotary phones?

Was Bill willingly playing Sancho Panza to John's Don Quixote? Or was an intervention in order?

I was assured by my friend that Bill likely knew exactly what he was doing — as, of course, he always did.

So I contacted Bill and offered to help out, thinking he would ask for a check. He did — but he also issued a challenge: "Perhaps you could also write a kind of 'good olde days' column," he emailed, "but remembering the humor that you were once known for."

Bill was clever. What I heard was, "Waite, you flaccid, pathetic product of corporate excess and political equivocation, can you still hit a fastball (or at least look good while striking out)"?

Hence this weekly column.

My intent has been to do as Bill asked. But I not only try to anchor each column in a memory or contemporary event relating to Ipswich, but I endeavor to take things to a more universal level for a wider audience. As for remembering the humor I was once known for, I have tried ... despite these being profoundly unfunny times.

After more than 100 columns, I began getting requests to compile them — or at least some of them — into a book.

While I have co-authored a couple of books on personal finance and contributed a chapter to one titled "Conversations With John Updike," I had never been involved with the actual publication process. To my mind, book publishing could be likened to bratwurst-making — I enjoy the finished product, but I would prefer to stay far from the process that brings it into my hands.

Plus, aren't books also dead?

It seems they are not. People are still buying books, in both print and eBook format. So I decided to plunge ahead.

Fortunately, I have a brother, Tom, who is no stranger to publishing. He has five best-selling thrillers under his belt and has navigated the world of Amazon and Kindle.

He offered up his imprint — Marlborough Press, named after the street in the Back Bay — and his tag-team of associates, including Asha Hossain, a designer who specializes in book covers.

I had two thoughts regarding a cover. Ipswich photographer Stoney Stone, whose work I admire immensely, had generously offered to let me use one of his shots. And I also owned a painting, "Walking the Beach," by Ipswich artist Colleen Kidder, that I also thought might work.

Asha loved the photographs but urged me to use the painting, which she felt worked better for the response she was trying to evoke.

I also engaged a formatter, a fellow named Dallas Hodge. Yes, books need to be formatted, both for eBook and printed versions. Dallas, who lives in Texas (but not in Dallas) suggested a font called "Glacial Indifference" for my particular work. A music teacher by trade, his recommendation hit just the right note for me.

The book is now out. Called *Ipswich On My Mind*, it is available from Amazon and as a Kindle eBook. All of the proceeds will go directly to *Ipswich Local News* to support quality community journalism. (I had originally thought to devote the profits, but my brother pointed out that, after expenses, there probably won't be any profits!)

In some small way, I would like to think I am honoring the late Bill Wasserman's call to action … and John Muldoon's vision. If I hit a few singles along the way, so much the better.

(Bob Waite also considered* Tarbox Secrets Revealed *as the book's title but feared being sued by Alfred A. Knopf.)

Acknowledgments

I want to begin by thanking my brother Tom for allowing me to nestle under his Marlborough Press imprint once again and to continue to engage e-book and print formatter Dallas Hodge and cover designer Asha Hossain. Both are an absolute pleasure.

I also want to thank Stephanie Gaskins, President of the Ipswich Museum, for granting me permission to use an Arthur Wesley Dow painting, "Ipswich Shanties", for the book's cover. The high-resolution image of the painting was shot by one of my favorite photographers, Stoney Stone.

The story behind the cover image is an interesting one – I actually had two Arthur Wesley Dow paintings to choose from. The other was "The Derelict" (pictured), which was offered by the Museum of the American Arts and Crafts Movement (MAACM) of St. Petersburg, FL. In that regard I wish to thank the Museum's founder and President, Rudy Ciccarello, for his generosity – and I promise to use their image in a future book.

In the meantime, I would urge anyone who happens to be in the neighborhood of the MAACM to visit this wonderful treasure trove of Americana.

I want to thank my loyal Ipswich retailers, Betsy Frost of Betsy Frost Designs; Mike McGrath of Zenobia; and Margaret Morley of the Ipswich Inn. They have not only carried my books, but have hosted signings and talks (or, in the case of the Ipswich Inn, hosted me for the night).

I am fortunate to have a retinue of friends, some stretching so far back into my childhood that they still reference me as "Bobby", to call upon to help me jog my memory. They include Stacey Pedrick, Ann Herrick Causey, Kathleen Hayes Garland, David Grimes, Michael McSweeney, Jeff Dolan, Mike Girard, David Benedix, Janet Mackay-Smith, Sharon Kennedy, Anthony Pappas, and Neil Cleary, just to name a few.

Thanks also to Ipswich Town Historian Gordon Harris; to Ipswich Public Library Director Nora Blake and her fine staff, including Reference Librarian Katy Wuerker; and ever-helpful town officials, including Town Clerk Amy Akell, Town Assessor Mary-Louise Ireland, and Select Board member Charlie Surpitski.

Wayne Castonguay and Susan Winthrop continue to be very helpful in shaping my understanding of environmental issues, most particularly as they relate to the Ipswich River.

A special note of thanks to Clark Norton, my former editor at Pacific News Service, for allowing me to use two of my previously published travel articles, which first appeared on his renowned Baby-Boomer Travel site.

As a regular contributor to *Ipswich Local News* I am fortunate to be in the company of a gaggle of fine columnists, including Doug Brendel, Bill Sargent, Esther Baird, Paula Jones, and Rebecca Pugh. I am humbled by their talent and enthusiasm. I am also privileged to operate under the watchful eye of Editor and Publisher John P. Muldoon and his ever-helpful partner, Deputy Editor Kristen Aiton Muldoon.

Finally, my deep appreciation to my wife of more than 35 years, Karen Shigeishi-Waite, who has not only put up with me, but has heard many of my stories so many times that she can tell them better than I can.

Other Fine Books Available From Marlborough Press

"Ipswich On My Mind", Bob Waite

"Shadowed", Thomas Waite

"Terminal Value", Thomas Waite

"Unholy Code: A Lana Elkins Thriller", Thomas Waite

https://thomaswaite.com

About the Author

Ipswich native Bob Waite began his writing career in 1970 with the *Ipswich Chronicle* and other North Shore Weeklies newspapers as summer reporter and editor. During that time he won three New England Press Association best column awards. He subsequently worked for Pacific News Service (PNS), covering U.S. politics from San Francisco, and as PNS' Eastern European Correspondent, based in Warsaw, Poland. He later served as press secretary to Senators Edward W. Brooke and Robert J. Dole.

Following his government stint, Bob moved to the corporate sector and led communications, marketing, and government relations functions at IBM, Ford, CAE, Inc., CIBC, and Canada Post. He is currently a professor at Seneca Polytechnic in Toronto and Managing Director of Waite + Co., a communications strategy firm.

Bob returned to his journalistic roots in 2020 as a columnist for *Ipswich Local News*. In addition, he writes frequently on travel for a baby boomer-oriented travel site managed by Clark Norton one of his former PNS editors.

Although Bob now physically resides in Ontario, Canada, and his Ipswich family home passed to others in 2006, he has retained his Ipswich citizenship - and his South Side sensibilities.